Reiki: 200 Q&A
for Beginners

Lawrence Ellyard

Author of 'Reiki Healer'

Founder of the International Institute for Reiki Training

www.reikitraining.com.au

BOOKS

Winchester, U.K.
New York, U.S.A.

First published by O Books, 2006
An imprint of John Hunt Publishing Ltd., The Bothy, Deershot
Lodge, Park Lane, Ropley, Hants, SO24 oBE, UK
office@johnhunt-publishing.com
www.o-books.net

USA and Canada	Singapore
NBN	STP
custserv@nbnbooks.com	davidbuckland@tlp.com.sg
Tel: 1 800 462 6420	Tel: 65 6276
Fax: 1 800 338 4550	Fax: 65 6276 7119
Australia	**South Africa**
Brumby Books	Alternative Books
sales@brumbybooks.com	altbook@global.co.za
Tel: 61 3 9761 5535	Tel: 27 011 792 7730
Fax: 61 3 9761 7095	Fax: 27 011 972 7787

New Zealand
Peaceful Living
books@peaceful-living.co.nz
Tel: 64 09 921 6222
Fax: 64 09 921 6220

Text copyright Lawrence Ellyard 2006
Design: Jim Weaver Design, Basingstoke
Cover design: Infograf Ltd, London

ISBN 1 905047 47 9

A CIP catalogue record for this book is available from the British
Library.

Printed by CPI Antony Rowe, Chippenham, UK

Contents

Authors note   xiii
Introduction – How to use this book   xiv
Dedication   xv

1 New to Reiki, the basics revealed   1

  1 What is Reiki?
  2 What does the word Reiki mean?
  3 What does Reiki heal and how does it work?
  4 What is a Reiki attunement?
  5 Can I heal myself with Reiki?
  6 How many Reiki degrees are there?
  7 Is Reiki Buddhist and does one need to become a Buddhist to learn Reiki?
  8 How much does it cost to learn Reiki?
  9 What are some of the benefits of learning Reiki?
  10 What attracts people to Reiki?
  11 Is Reiki always safe?
  12 What are dualistic forms of energy?
  13 From a Reiki perspective, why do people get sick?
  14 Do I gain any qualifications from learning Reiki?
  15 Is Reiki a spiritual tradition?
  16 What are the factors which determine the best kind of connection to the Reiki energy?
  17 Is Reiki a form of Channelling?

2 Receiving Reiki   19

  18 Do I have to be ill to receive Reiki?
  19 What does one experience during a treatment?
  20 How should I feel after a treatment?

21 Is there anything I should do to support myself after a treatment?

22 Do I need to remove any clothing before a treatment?

23 Is it normal to experience feeling emotional during or after a Reiki treatment?

24 What are some of the ways that I can support myself when emotions arise?

25 What are some ways to transform these emotions?

26 When receiving Reiki, why does my body twitch and jolt from time to time?

27 Why do the practitioners hands get hot during treatments?

28 Is Reiki always experienced as heat through the hands?

29 Why do some people's tummy's rumble during a treatment?

3   The Reiki Styles, Lineage, and History   31

30 What is a Reiki lineage and is a lineage in Reiki important?

31 Is it possible to have more than one Reiki lineage?

32 What is the difference between tradition and non-traditional Reiki?

33 What are the main Reiki lineages available today?

34 How old is Reiki and from where did it originate?

35 Who founded Reiki?

36 Do any of Usui's original manuscripts remain intact today?

37 Was Usui a Christian or a Buddhist?

4   Before learning Reiki   41

38 How do I find a suitable Reiki teacher?

39 Can one learn Reiki online or solely from books?

40 Are psychic abilities a part of Reiki?

41 What should I do to prepare myself before taking a Reiki class?

42 If I feel heat in my hands, without the Reiki attunements, does this mean that I have Reiki or is this some other form of energy?

43 Is Reiki just for the gifted or can anyone learn?

44 Are some people better at doing Reiki than others?

45 Will Reiki work on someone who is not receptive to it?

46 Which types of abilities will I have after learning the First Degree in Reiki?

47 How long does a Reiki treatment last?

5 Reiki and its effects 51

48 Can someone who is physically disabled learn Reiki?

49 Can someone who is mentally disabled learn Reiki?

50 Can someone learn Reiki who is suffering from a Mental illness?

51 Does Reiki work every time?

52 Why can't everyone just do Reiki without formal instruction?

53 How many treatments does a person require before they are healed?

54 How do drugs and alcohol affect the Reiki energy?

55 Is a group Reiki treatment better that one person giving a treatment?

56 How many treatments can a Reiki practitioner give before they become drained of their life force energy?

57 Is Reiki always facilitated with the hands above the body or on the body?

6 First Degree Reiki 57

58 How important is faith and intent when giving Reiki?

59 How long does it take to become a practitioner of Reiki?

60 Can Reiki wear out and can you over energise someone with Reiki?

61 What are the Reiki hand positions?

62 Do Reiki practitioners use a code of ethics and is there an international standard of practice?

63 What are the Reiki Principles and where did they come from?

64 Should I charge for Reiki and if so, how much?

65 How often do I need to practice to maintain the Reiki energy?

66 Is there any time where Reiki would not be safe?

67 What are Reiki Guides and do I need to know my guides to learn Reiki?

7   Reiki experiences and the Chakras   71

68   Why do some people who receive Reiki experience various colours?
69   What does it mean when someone's body twitches during a treatment?
70   What does it mean when my eyes flutter during a Reiki treatment?
71   When I give Reiki, why do I feel the need to yawn?
72   What are the Chakras and how do these relate to Reiki?
73   Is there only one system of the Chakras?
74   How can I balance the Chakras with Reiki energy?
75   Can I balance my own Chakras with Reiki?
76   How long should I wait between Reiki levels?

8   The Reiki Attunements   79

77   How do the Reiki attunements work?
78   Can people receive a connection to Reiki without the Attunements?
79   How many attunements are given throughout the entire Reiki system?
80   What does one experience during an attunement?
81   What happens during the initiations and why do I have my eyes closed?
82   What if I don't feel anything during the attunements?
83   What is the difference between a Reiki attunement and a Reiki treatment in terms of energy transference?
84   Is there a way to give yourself a Reiki attunement?
85   What role does ritual play in attunements?
86   What does a Reiki teacher experience when giving the attunements?
87   What are the differences between the First, Second and Third Degree attunements?
88   What role do the Chakras play in the attunement process?
89   How do the attunements affect the human energy field?
90   What is the 21-day integration process?
91   If I have learnt Reiki elsewhere and receive an attunement with another teacher, will this cancel out my previous Reiki attunement?

92 How is Reiki energy different to other energy healing
systems?

93 How does Reiki energy blend with other energy healing
systems?

94 If I receive the Reiki attunements whilst pregnant, will my
child be born with Reiki?

9 Giving Reiki to others   Part 1   **93**

95 Can I pick up another's symptoms whilst giving Reiki?

96 How can I identify this kind of transference?

97 Is there a way of purifying the client's lower energies
when normal Reiki healing is not sufficient?

98 What are some ways to cleanse myself after a Reiki
treatment?

99 What use has salt in cleaning lower energies?

100 Can Reiki accelerate the bodies healing rate and if so,
how does this work?

101 What does it mean, when someone does not heal?

102 What if the person has the wish to be well, and has
received several treatments, but no matter how many,
the illness still remains?

103 Are there any contra-indications to the use of Reiki?

104 Can a practitioner transfer their own negativity to the
client during a treatment?

105 Are there some ways to create personal boundaries in
healing work?

106 Is it necessary to remove jewellery before a treatment, and
can jewellery interfere with the flow of healing energy?

107 What are some guidelines for practitioners when treating
others?

108 How do I know when to move my hands to another
position during a treatment?

109 Why is it that both the practitioner and the client can
become thirsty during and proceeding a Reiki treatment?

10 Giving Reiki to others   Part 2   **105**

110 Why do I sometimes feel comfortable receiving Reiki from
one practitioner whilst not as comfortable with another?

111 What can I do if I feel an aversion to another and what are some ways to look at this?

112 How can I increase sensitivity in my hands for healing myself and others?

113 Is there a way to sense imbalances in the energy field?

114 When giving Reiki, why can one side feel stronger than the other?

115 What is some advice for treating people with serious illnesses?

116 Will my mundane thoughts interfere with the flow of Reiki energy?

117 Is there a mantra that I can use with Reiki to heal myself and others?

118 Why does Reiki feel different from one treatment to the next on the same person?

119 Does it matter which hand goes left or right when giving a treatment?

120 How important is posture when giving Reiki?

11 Giving Reiki to others Part 3   115

121 What kind of pressure do I need to apply to my hands when giving Reiki to another?

122 Should I keep my fingers closed or open whilst giving Reiki to myself or others, and is there a difference in energy flow?

123 If I feel the need to move my hands above the body or back and forth during a treatment, should I do this?

124 How can I ground my energy after giving or receiving a Reiki treatment?

125 Do I need to give Reiki for as long to a small child as I would with an adult?

126 Why is it that during a Reiki seminar or in Reiki share groups, my energy feels strong, yet when I am alone, I do not feel as much?

127 Is there a way to give healing at a distance at the beginner's level?

128 How important is Practice? If I don't practice will Reiki stop working?

129 Is receiving a group Reiki treatment more powerful than from one person and how does this affect the outcomes?

12 Reiki and its extended applications **123**

130 Can I give myself Reiki to go to sleep and will Reiki keep on working when I fall asleep?

131 How could I use Reiki in a First Aid situation?

132 Is it advisable to give Reiki to someone who has been bitten or stung by something venomous?

133 Can Reiki be used during pregnancy?

134 I heard you should not give Reiki to a pregnant woman, is this correct?

135 Can Reiki be used to alleviate the symptoms of period pain?

136 Can I energize food and water with the Reiki energy and what effect does it have?

137 Does Reiki work on non-living objects, and can you recharge batteries with Reiki energy?

138 Is it possible to give Reiki to animals and can animals do Reiki or be attuned to the energy?

139 What do I do if either my client or I experience sexual feelings during a treatment?

140 Can Reiki heal issues of sexual trauma?

141 Can Reiki be used between lovers to enhance intimacy?

13 Reiki and Spirituality **135**

142 What is Karma?

143 How do we create Karma?

144 Are people who do Reiki in this life, doing this because they were healers in former lives?

145 If a client has an illness due to past karma and it is their karmic path to experience their illness, by attempting to heal that person are we interfering with that progress?

146 Do I need to change my diet or become a vegetarian to practice Reiki?

147 What are some of the long term abilities which arise from long term Reiki practice?

14 Second Degree Questions **143**

148 How does one determine whether one is ready to learn the Second Degree?

149   Are Reiki practitioners required to have insurance in order to practice?

150   Can someone who has learnt a different Reiki style pick up a new Reiki style from a different teacher or does one need to review previous levels?

151   Should I wait until I am completely healed before healing others?

152   Can Reiki be used to heal the environment?

153   Can Reiki assist with healing relationships?

154   What general guidelines are recommended for setting up a Reiki practice?

155   Can Reiki be used to protect me from harmful circumstances?

156   How can I use Reiki to heal emotions like anger?

157   How do I know if a session has worked if no visible signs are apparent?

158   Can Reiki be used as the sole method of treatment for serious illness?

159   Can one energise Western Medicine with Reiki energy?

15   Reiki Symbols Questions   157

160   What are the Reiki symbols?

161   Why are symbols used in Reiki?

162   How are the Reiki symbols used in healing?

163   Can anyone use the Reiki symbols for healing without initiation into Reiki?

164   Can I use the Reiki symbols to protect myself?

165   What are the names of the Reiki symbols?

166   Can you tell me some of the Power symbol uses in Reiki?

167   Can you tell me more of the Harmony symbol uses in Reiki?

168   Can you tell me more of the Connection symbol uses in Reiki?

169   Why are the Reiki symbols shrouded in secrecy?

170   What are non-traditional Reiki symbols?

171   Are non-traditional Reiki symbols as effective as the traditional ones?

172   Can the Reiki symbols increase the amount of Reiki energy transferred in healing?

173 How important is it to have the correct renderings of the Reiki symbols?

174 Do the Reiki symbols have a power of their own, or is it the Practitioner's faith in them which activates the power?

175 Can the Reiki symbols lose their power if you show them to someone who is not initiated into the Second Degree?

16 Distant Healing   169

176 What is Distant healing?

177 Is there more than one way to do distant healing?

178 If I take my hands off the effigy or if my concentration is disturbed, will this stop the distant healing?

179 Do I need to use the same effigy for distant healing?

180 Can distant healing be harmful if the person receiving it has not given their consent?

181 Is distant healing stronger than hands-on healing?

182 Can I give Reiki to someone who has died?

183 Can I send Reiki energy into the future?

184 Can I send Reiki energy into the past to heal my present issues?

185 Can I send healing to every year of my life and how do I do this?

186 Can I send Reiki healing to more than one person at a time?

187 How can I use distant healing to manifest my goals?

188 Can I work on more than one issue at a time when giving a distant healing?

17 Reiki Mastery   181

189 Is everyone who is a Reiki Master a teacher of Reiki?

190 What is a Reiki Master Teacher?

191 What is a Reiki Grand Master?

192 What is the Master symbol?

193 How is the Third degree symbol used in Reiki?

194 Can Reiki Masters give attunements without symbols?

195 How quickly can a Reiki Master teach a student to be a Reiki Master?

196 Is there such a thing as group Reiki attunements?

197   Is there a global Reiki community or international head to Reiki?

198   Is there a difference between a Reiki Master and a Reiki Instructor and what is a Reiki Sensei?

199   Do Reiki Masters get sick or does their Reiki ability prevent illness?

200   Can Reiki Masters avert their own Karma?

Appendix   189

About the IIRT   189

About the Author   189

Recommended Reiki Websites   189

Recommended Reiki Books   190

Contact Details   191

Author's note

Reiki: 200 Q&A for Beginners, was written in such a way to give the reader a step into the Reiki classroom and to acquaint oneself with some of the common and perhaps not so commonly asked questions about Reiki. Throughout these pages you will encounter several topics on Reiki. From questions and answers to a variety of Reiki experiences; to the inner meanings of the Reiki attunements, this book expounds all of the answers to the questions that can arise by either giving or receiving Reiki.

Introduction – How to use this book

Reiki: 200 Q&A for Beginners is not only a book to read from start to finish, it is a guide to the complete way and practice of Reiki. This book is not meant to replace the teacher, however, by utilising the contents list of questions, in all but a few cases your question and the answer will be found.

Each chapter is categorised by topics. For example, if you have a general question about Reiki attunements or the Reiki symbols, then a chapter is devoted for each topic. If on the other hand you have a question about a particular Reiki experience, then chapters 9 through 11 will present your answer.

It is my hope that this book will satisfy your Reiki curiosity and will remain of lasting benefit in your practice and journey with Reiki.

Yours in Reiki
Lawrence Ellyard

Dedication

This book is dedicated to all Reiki students everywhere.
Without your questions this book would never have been written.

1

New to Reiki – the Basics revealed

1 | What is Reiki?

Reiki is a method of hands on healing which originated in Japan at the turn of the 20th Century. It is a system of healing that transforms and heals the body and mind. Utilizing the methods within the Reiki system, the Reiki practitioner transfers healing energy via the hands to another.

Reiki energy is the healing energy of the Universe. It represents a matrix of non-dualistic energy, which permeates all things. A Reiki practitioner harnesses this vital energy via a series of attunements, which in effect, switch on the ability to transfer Reiki energy to oneself and others.

The transmission of this energy comes via a Reiki teacher, someone who knows the precise methods for creating this alignment within the practitioner. Once this alignment is complete, the practitioner can then use this healing energy in a variety of ways to restore the body, mind and emotions into a harmonious state.

Reiki has beneficial results for those who give, as well as those who receive it. It creates an avenue for healing which includes healing the primary cause of illness as well as its physical manifestations.

2 | What does the word Reiki Mean?

Reiki is essentially broken down into two parts: "Rei" and "Ki". Rei represents: Universal, Spirit, mystery and gift. And Ki represents

Energy, life force, talent and feeling. These two parts combined form the word or 'Kanji', which represents universal life force energy. So Reiki is a union with the 'Universal Spirit' and your life force energy and in many respects describes what actually occurs when someone is practicing Reiki.

Mikao Usui, the founder of Reiki described the word Reiki as Rei, representing Divine healing energy and Ki, representing life force energy, both of the individual and of the universe.

The kanji characters Rei and Ki both have an old (Fig. 1) and a modern (Fig. 2) form.

Figure 1   *Figure 2*

When examining the older form we gain a deeper insight into Reiki and its inner meaning. The kanji of Reiki in effect describes the process of Reiki and the relationship one forms with the energy.

The modern depiction of the kanji Reiki is somewhat limited and much of the original meaning has been removed to simply convey a two-part image.

The older style of kanji better describes Usui's description of the system and illustrates the inner spiritual meaning, particularly the upper portion of the symbol.

Rei – Has 24 strokes to the kanji, and consists of 3 parts. The top part represents the descent of rain, or in this case the descent of Universal Healing energy. The middle part represents three open mouths, and bottom represents the recipient of this rain or the worthy aspirant receiving the universal healing energies.

If we examine a modern day Japanese dictionary, Rei is defined as:

(1) Spirit, the spiritual aspect of the human being as contrasted to the physical. (2) Divine, luminous, charismatic, supernatural, mysterious. (3) The luminosity of the spirit, the luminosity of a God or Sage. (4) Inconceivable spiritual ability; charismatic power; charisma; wonderful, a wonder. (5) A rainmaker, a diviner; a person or being with spiritual or supernatural powers. (6) A shaman. (7) Goodness; good, excellent, efficacious. (8) Clever, nimble, sharp. (9) Life. (10) A living being, a human being. (11) A supernatural (mythical) beast or being; a fairy, an elf. (12) Pure, undefined, unpolluted. (13) Bright, clear.

Ki – Has 10 strokes to the kanji and consists of the symbols of breath with rice. (Rice in Japan is sometimes used as a synonym for people). Ki, then in this case represents "energy" of beings.

The Japanese dictionary defines Ki as: (1) vital energy connected with the breath. Invisible life force, somewhat equivalent to 'Prana'. (2) The generative forces of heaven and earth, by means of which all things are constantly reproduced. (3) Air. (4) Breath, steam.

Other similar representations of Ki energy can be found in various cultures. The Chinese call this energy 'Chi' or 'Qi', the Hindu tradition refer to this energy as 'Prana', the Sufi tradition refer to is as 'Baraka' while ancient healing traditions of Egypt refer to this energy as 'Ka'. However, these names only indicate the energy of Ki and do not refer to the whole experience that is Reiki, being the union of Universe and humankind.

In China, another word, which bears a similar expression, is 'Ling Qi'. In China, 'Ling', refers to the animating force or power of the universe and Qi, the medium for its manifestation in the physical plane. As Japan inherited the Chinese characters for its use of language, the thread of meaning in these forms is present to some extent however one often requires a sound understanding of the old style kanji to find this relationship.

If we were to describe Reiki with its spiritual meaning, the characters form the following picture: Upon the earth stands a human being, with arms raised to the heavens. From the heavens rain descends, bringing the healing energies of the Universe and bestowing this blessing upon the being. This being is now a conduit or channel, bestowing the life giving energy to all humanity.

In this way, the kanji of Reiki reveals much about our relationship to Reiki. It is a picture, which tells of our union between our own energy and the energy of the universe.

3 | What does Reiki heal and how does it work?

Reiki is a unique healing system, which can be applied to almost any physical ailment with positive results.

Reiki can be applied to any part of the body, injury or illness. It also has a calming effect on the mind and emotions. On the physical level, Reiki can be applied to the physical body, including all of the conditions, which concern the body. Anything from a headache to sore muscles. From period pain, to healing emotional stress, Reiki can be applied in numerous ways. The possibilities are endless.

On the emotional level, Reiki can be of assistance with its nurturing ability to soothe and pacify negative emotions, such as anger, fear, anxiety, pride, ignorance and depression. Primarily, Reiki has immediate benefits for calming stress and tension, whether this is an outer manifestation in the body, or the mental and emotional causes to the physical condition.

Perhaps the best way to describe Reiki is to consider our bodies much like forms of energy and light. The way we interact with our environment and with others, as well as our actions, thoughts and established patterns, all determine the harmonious function of our energy body. All of these factors are interrelated and determine whether our experience is of health and balance or ill health and stress.

One can describe Reiki's ability to heal as a subtle energy matrix. Each of us has a specific vibrational rate. Due to our previous actions or 'Karma', this vibrational rate becomes out of tune. When this happens, the result is illness. Reiki thereby works by re-attuning the bodies' own vibrational rate to that of a healthy and harmonious vibration. By bestowing the healing energy, which was missing due to past wrong actions, our mental state of being and our physical illness, we restore a state of balance and renewed vitality.

When Reiki energy is administered in the form of a treatment through a qualified practitioner, the practitioner simply acts as a conduit for these healing energies to transfer through himself or herself to the recipient. This healing energy activates the recipients own healing process, giving the body (in particular the energy body) the ability to heal itself by receiving a natural boost of life force energy through the practitioner administering the treatment.

4 What is a Reiki attunement?

The Reiki attunements are the energy alignments a teacher of Reiki gives to a student. In various schools and styles of Reiki the ways these attunements are given to the student vary in approach and methodology. However, irrespective of differences in methodology, in most cases each attunement activates an ability to use Reiki energy for oneself and others almost immediately.

If we were to use an analogy of what an attunement is, then we might think that the Reiki energy is a radio signal, our energy body a radio and our radio antenna or receiver the body's energy system. When a teacher adjusts our antenna (by tuning in our dials or Chakras) we effectively pick up the station 'Reiki' and as a result, any previous static that was found on our station is removed and a clear reception is found. Thus the ability to channel Reiki energy is bestowed.

Another amazing thing about this system is one need not believe in Reiki for it to work. Thus ruling out a placebo effect, the Reiki healing ability can be successfully bestowed to anyone.

The actual Reiki attunement is a small ceremony, which creates this alignment. Many attunement procedures make use of symbols particular to the system and these are drawn by the teacher into various places of energy flow in the recipient's body. The symbols act like keys. Much like opening a door, these symbols open new pathways of energy, which were previously laying dormant or 'locked up' in the persons' energy system. For a detailed explanation of the attunement process see Chapter 8 – The Reiki attunements.

5 Can I heal myself with Reiki?

From the outset, many people think Reiki is a method for healing others, yet many are pleasantly surprised to hear that one can effectively use Reiki for self-healing. Many methods exist in the various Reiki styles for self-healing. The most common form of Reiki self-healing is the direct application of ones' hands on oneself and allowing Reiki energy to flow to the areas where the hands are in contact. In many western Reiki traditions, this simple practice uses a standard placement of the hands on the body to cover all the major organs of the body and areas of energy flow. One places their hands on these areas for 3 to 5 minutes and this is all that is required. In other Reiki styles, practitioners utilize their minds to focus their awareness by consciously directing Reiki energy in specific ways.

For example, in the Japanese Reiki style, many of Mikao Usui's original techniques are given, ranging from meditation, breathing exercises, body movement, the use of sound and mantras, as well as visualization techniques to enhance the energy flow within and outside the physical body. No matter the style used, the effects of self-healing are easy to obtain and actually require little effort on behalf of the practitioner. As Reiki is simply activated by touch, the practitioner need only place their hands on his or her body to receive the healing benefits.

6 | How many Reiki degrees are there?

Reiki is essentially broken into degrees or stages. These again vary depending upon the particular Reiki style and system. In most lineages of Reiki, there are three degrees. These include: First Degree (beginners level), Second Degree (advanced level), and Third Degree (teacher level). However in some schools, these levels have additional stages and may be taught in as little as a few days, to a series of weeks, months or even years.

In the Japanese Reiki system of the *Usui Reiki Ryoho Gakkai* (learning society), their Reiki system is broken down into the following stages:

- Shoden (level 1 or beginning teachings)
- Okuden (level 2 or practitioner)
- Shinpiden (level 3 or teaching level)

In some Japanese Reiki schools the levels count from level 6, down to level 1. Much in the same way that one progresses though a series of grades in martial arts training.

A school of Reiki taught by Kyozou Ogawa in Japan offers 6 levels or stages. The highest level available is Okuden Koeki or level 1. When a capable student is invited to take the Shinpiden or teacher training level they learn the methods of how to teach the information and techniques, as well as the attunements for all 6 levels of Reiki.

The following are the levels taught:

- Level 6 – Dai Loku Tou – Shoden level ('Beginning teachings')
- Level 5 – Dai Go Tou – Shoden level
- Level 4 – Dai Yon Tou – Shoden level
- Level 3 – Dai San Tou – Shoden level
- Level 2 – Okuden Zenki – Okuden first term
- Level 1 – Okuden Koeki – Okuden latter term ('Highest or secret level')
- Teaching Level – Shinpiden – ('Ultimate secret method')

In recent times, much information has come forth from Japan regarding how the original Reiki Society teaches Reiki (*The Reiki Gakkai*). This school incorporates the use of particular 'ranks for proficiency.'

These ranks are based on the student's ability to channel Reiki energy and their adeptness or proficiency in performing the particular techniques given at each stage. A student will go from proficiency rank 6 ('the beginning level' or First Degree) where the student learns hand-on and other techniques from the Shoden level; and make their way gradually through the fifth and fourth stages.

It is not until the student attains the third proficiency rank the Okuden (or Second Degree) that advanced techniques like distance healing are offered. In some cases, it can take a student as long as 10 years before attaining the Shinpiden level (sensei).

For many western students who are used to taking a weekend workshop to learn Reiki first degree, this might seem a bit extreme, however this way of learning is based on the sound integration and accomplishment of the methods learnt in each level. In a similar way as one would learn a language, students meet weekly and build on their previous experience through the practical application of the methods within the system.

Although Reiki is often dismissed as merely being a system of hands-on healing, it is in fact a complete method or path to reaching higher levels of spiritual consciousness. In this way, healing is seen as a step that occurs on the way to enlightenment. Unfortunately, many of the higher and less well known spiritual practices are missing from many modern day Reiki styles and these days it becomes harder to find an authentic teacher who can pass on this knowledge.

In other systems of Reiki, the teacher level or third degree is broken into two stages these being, stage A and stage B. Also referred to as '3A and 3B'. Stage A consists of learning the Mastery symbol, a symbol which is used to attune others into Reiki as well as advanced methods of energy work, and stage B takes the form of an apprenticeship where all attunement procedures are taught as well as training on how to run classes for students who wish to learn.

The Radiance technique, (a derivative of Reiki, which sprang forth from the teachings of Mrs. Takata), has a completely different progression of levels. This system was developed by Dr. Barbara Ray who was a student of the late Mrs. Takata, professes to teach seven higher levels which were not revealed to any of Mrs. Takata's other students. Although there is no evidence of a seven level system in any of the older and more traditional Reiki styles in Japan, the Radiance Technique, like many others, works none the less. Many Reiki styles have varied approaches to learning and this has no bearing on the effectiveness or ineffectiveness of the system itself. What are important are the methodology and how one utilises these methods to benefit oneself and others.

As with each style of Reiki, the progression from one level to the next, should emphasise personal integration and practice of the methods taught before taking a new level within a system. This is true to say for most things, as one does not gain a high level of accomplishment and experience in a short time. Practice is just as important as knowledge. They go hand in hand to bring experience and integration of the Reiki methods and the ways to gaining personal transformation.

7   Is Reiki Buddhist and does one need to become a Buddhist to learn Reiki?

The way Reiki is taught today all around the world is a melting pot of many things.

Although the original Reiki system was based on Buddhist Sutra and Tantra, as well as being inspired and developed by Usui who was a devout Buddhist, the way of Reiki does not require formal Buddhist commitments. Usui also studied many other religious systems of his day, and these studies flavoured his system of healing. Usui was very interested in benefiting as many beings as possible with his system and during his teaching career he made Reiki available to anyone, regardless of their religious persuasions. Depending upon which style and teacher one chooses to study with, one can encounter any number of views and religious influences introduced to Reiki. Thus it can become quite confusing for someone who is considering a teacher and Reiki style.

8 How much does it cost to learn Reiki?

What one pays for Reiki will vary tremendously depending on which teacher you decide upon. The importance is not always on how much you pay, (though very high fees should not be tolerated) but what you will be receiving when learning Reiki. It is better to think of Reiki as an important investment for your health. Learning Reiki is an investment that will not only benefit the health of your body, but the health of your mind. When we consider this, then learning Reiki takes on a whole new meaning.

One can learn Reiki for a reasonable fee and when making the decision to learn from a teacher, choose a reputable one, as this person is responsible for awakening your Reiki ability. Therefore a person who has some sound experience and a good motivation in their own Reiki practice is ideal.

The very idea of paying to learn Reiki is an important one. If you pay too little, you may not value what you have received. On the other hand, if you pay too much, this may cause untold burdens in your life as you struggle to get by. For some, 150 US dollars is nothing, for others this fee represents months of scrimping and saving.

Of the many Reiki styles available, the Reiki Alliance is one of the few Reiki styles which formed a fee structure around Reiki. A teacher of this style charges $150 US for Reiki, First Degree, $500 US for Reiki, Second Degree, and $10,000 US for Reiki, Third Degree. This amount is paid by each student per level, regardless of which country and the relative strength of the currency in that country where one resides.

Now most people's reactions to paying $10,000 US for Reiki Third Degree are understandably, quite bewildering, least of all basing an amount on US currency. However this is but one formal fee structure and most Reiki teachers world-wide do not ascribe to this.

On the flip side, some Reiki teachers do not put a price on Reiki classes and consider charging these kinds of fees inappropriate, yet others still, practice Reiki as a livelihood making it necessary to charge a fee.

When we offer healing to another or a system of healing for that matter, it is important that some form of exchange occurs. Be this in the form of barter, money or goods and services, the giver has expended energy and the one who receives it should balance this by some form of exchange.

Today most teachers of Reiki charge a reasonable fee, which is based on their time, expertise and effort for giving a class. Time is money as they say and what you pay for is the teacher's time. Paying for a service also represents a symbolic trust in the teachings.

9 | What are some of the benefits of learning Reiki?

The benefits of learning Reiki are many and the Reiki system provides such a large scope of possibilities. Hopefully by reading this book you'll see the enormous potential of Reiki and its benefits, but here is an overview of some of the key points.

- Reiki not only heals the physical body, it works towards healing the cause of illness, thereby eliminating the effects of the imbalance.
- Reiki lasts a lifetime. Once you have the attunements, regardless of whether you use the energy consciously or not, it is always with you.
- Reiki can be successfully combined with other healing methods and is a useful tool to have, which can be incorporated into daily life.
- It does not conflict with religious beliefs therefore it is a teaching that can be used by anyone.
- Reiki is a self-empowering healing method. One has the ability to heal oneself and to generate greater self-reliance, which leads to independence. It is also an alternative, natural healing method, which is an additional way to heal the body and mind.
- Reiki promotes the qualities of love and compassion. With ongoing use a deep peace begins to permeate your life, anger begins to subside and more meaningful relationships endure.
- Reiki is an intelligent energy. It goes to the greatest need for the highest good of all concerned.
- Reiki begins to flow when you touch something; it's always on. Think of all the things you touch each day, then think of how Reiki could be of benefit.
- Reiki does not interfere with western medicine; it actually enhances medications, and assists the body to heal at an optimum rate.
- Reiki is an excellent tool for healing problems and for manifesting positive outcomes to numerous situations.
- Reiki can be used on animals, plants, children or any living being.
- Reiki calms nervous tension, calms fears and subdues negative emotions. It is also a useful technique for being guided and protected

throughout your life.
- Reiki is the highest form of healing energy, it is always safe and can never harm.
- It is available 24 hours a day, right there in your hands.

10 | What attracts people to Reiki?

In my experience, people come to Reiki when they are ready. Although, it would be more accurate to say that people come to Reiki when Reiki is ready to receive them. Learning Reiki can sometimes signal a time of transition for people and this is when most people actually take the step to arrange the necessary time in their life to learn.

As the saying goes: *"When the student is ready, the teacher appears".* When the student takes the step of learning Reiki a karmic connection between the student and the teacher begins. It is this connection which draws like minds together. There is no such thing as co-incidence and those who are ready to learn are guided to the correct teacher who can give them the appropriate methods for their journey. Today, all around the world there are millions of Reiki practitioners and hundreds of thousands of Reiki teachers. In the last 30 years, particularly, since 1988*, we have seen the number of Reiki teachers grow exponentially.

{* Up until 1988, Phyllis Lei Furumoto, the recognised head of the Reiki Alliance, was the only teacher within the Reiki Alliance who was recognised to initiate Reiki Masters. As the pressures of request grew in this position, Phyllis Lei Furumoto then announced that any suitably experienced Reiki Master could initiate another Master (teacher). This announcement in many ways opened the flood-gates, and a torrent of new Reiki Masters emerged within a few short years.}

The reason for such numbers of teachers and students is not just a matter of clever marketing this movement speaks of a greater need for more teachers and students of Reiki within the world. It seems there are more people than ever before, being "tapped on the shoulder" by Reiki to learn this way of healing.

11 | Is Reiki always safe?

Of the many things on offer in the spiritual and alternative health field, Reiki would have to be one of the most non-invasive, low impact and safest healing methods available. This is not only because receiving a treatment involves no manipulation of the physical body, it is also for the reason that the energy itself cannot cause an imbalance by either overuse or wrong application.

The practitioner simply places their hands gently on the body and the transference of healing energy passes from the practitioners' hands to the recipient, bringing about a calm and serene experience for both the giver and receiver.

Reiki works in flow with the bodies own ability to heal itself. By increasing the vital life force energy, the body is more able to draw on its own resources to fight off infection and to heal at a much faster rate. This has been demonstrated over and over in the speedy recovery of many illnesses and injuries. Another reason behind Reiki's safety is due to its non-dualistic vibration.

12 | What are dualistic forms of energy?

A dualistic form of energy is energy which can be used in a healing or harmful way. This is largely dependant upon the practitioners' intention, mental focus and level of experience.

For example, a dualistic energy is 'Chi'. Chi refers to raw life force energy. This energy requires a practitioner to have a good intention and mental focus to create a healing effect. For example, a martial arts expert can learn how to utilize Chi energy to strike a fatal blow to someone, or a Chinese Chi Kung Master might utilize the same energy with positive intent to heal an injury with a healing outcome.

When comparing other systems of healing, there are usually many rules concerning the application of energy. For example, one cannot energise sensitive organs, like the eyes, as the energy can have a damaging effect. Whereas one could energise the eyes with Reiki for hours and only benefit would ensue. Chi, Prana and other forms of energy work are powerful and therefore need to be controlled by the practitioner's intention to bring about safe results.

Reiki is a non-dualistic energy. The practitioner does not need to believe in it for it to work, nor do they need to focus their attention on the energy to obtain good results. Even the practitioners' thoughts, emotional or mental state, will have no adverse effect upon the Reiki energy being transferred to the person being treated. In fact, if a practitioner was experiencing disturbing emotions or stress in their own body, a large majority of these lower energies would actually be transformed by administering a Reiki treatment to someone else.

13   From a Reiki perspective, why do people get sick?

Perhaps the best way to look at illness is through our energy body. All illness manifests due to a maladjustment in our energy system. These maladjustments are caused by certain factors, which include:

- Our words, thoughts, and actions.
- Our previous Karma
- Our genetic proclivity
- The way we either nurture or harm our bodies
- Our energetic and physical environment

If we look at the first point, our thoughts and actions sow the seeds for our future. Our previous thoughts and actions currently influence our present state of health. As we think, so we become. If we do, think and say things which are harmful, we are sowing future harm for ourselves.

This brings us to our second point, our previous karma. The things we did, said and thought, sowed the seeds for our present circumstances. If we are experiencing illness and difficulty in our lives, it is due to our previous negative actions. This includes negative actions from former lives as well as this life.

The third point is our genetic proclivity. Our previous karma determines what type of body we have. We may have a body which is well, or a body which is subject to illness and injury. Our previous karma determines our parents and thereby what kind of gene pool we inherit.

The fourth point includes outer influences, including the types of food and drink we ingest. Certain foods and substances will have a good or harmful effect on our bodily systems. If we choose to harm our bodies through the over indulgence of these substances, we inevitably cause illness and harm.

The fifth point is our environment. Not only the physical exposure to certain chemicals, viruses and germs, but the energetic environments that we choose to live in. This also includes the people we live with, the friends we have as well as the kinds of work we do. All these have a direct effect on our health and peace of mind.

All of these factors affect the others and all have a karmic cause. If we are exposed to any of these lower vibrations, this in turn affects our energy body, which in turn creates illness, disharmony and disease.

To describe this in another way, we are much like a complex 'jig-saw' puzzle. When we are balanced and well, it is much like our puzzle is solved. All the parts are present and a complete picture of balance is revealed.

When we become ill, it is like some of the pieces are missing. Pieces go missing due to our mental state, our negative thoughts and actions. The very things we do, think and say affect our picture. When we do, think and say things, which are not beneficial, this creates a cause, which either manifests in our lives presently, or will be the seeds for future problems. When these negative actions ripen, illness and disharmony will be the result.

We can do much to prevent illness and misfortune in our lives. The application of Reiki restores the maladjustment to a state of balance and harmony, thus the symptoms and their causes are abated. One of the best ways to purify these obstacles is to give up harmful words, thoughts and actions and to replace these with positive words, thoughts and actions.

Reiki can become a central pillar to this. Through daily self-healing and meditations to purify the body and mind, we can do much to eradicate the karmic causes of illness. By healing others, we practice generosity, thus subduing our pride and increasing our own merit, which sows the seeds for a better future.

14 | Do I gain any qualifications from learning Reiki?

In many schools of Reiki, once you have attended a class or workshop you are issued with a certificate. Other schools offer an attendance certificate, which states the person has received the attunements and instructions for the particular level. What usually follows are a given number of practice hours and assessment. Provided the student has completed the necessary requirements, they are given a completion certificate which is part of the larger accreditation process. Here a student is often required to complete a number of logged treatments or clinical practices before they are issued with a certificate of completion. Often this is accompanied by a practicum and assessment with the Reiki Instructor to determine the student's level of proficiency.

Although many Reiki teachers do not offer any kind of formal practice and support after giving a class, there are those that do. This often takes the form of a 'Reiki share', where fellow Reiki students get together to practice on one another and to share in their experience and development.

As far as recognised certification, there are few Reiki schools that can offer government accredited courses that are recognised as an official qualification. Having said this, today some headway is being made to acknowledge Reiki as a recognised complementary therapy. The more people learn Reiki, the more the overall acceptance of Reiki will endure. Much in the same way that Chinese herbal medicine is now been used by some general practitioners. Perhaps in time, the merit of Reiki may be recognised in a similar fashion.

15 | Is Reiki a spiritual tradition?

To answer this question really depends on the individuals' concept of what is a spiritual tradition. Reiki originally stems from a long-standing spiritual tradition and indeed utilizes many practices.

If we consider a spiritual tradition as a method or series of practices which are passed down from a teacher to a student, who in turn become teachers themselves and in turn pass this onto their own students and so forth, then this would best describe the Reiki tradition. Reiki comes from a very old tradition, some sources stating the lineage goes back some 2500 years. It is also said that as the teaching moved from one culture to the next, as it is with one teacher to the next, each culture and person flavoured the teachings in unique ways.

Each person who becomes responsible for passing the tradition onto others (Reiki Teacher/Master), does so with the knowledge they possess. They pass their own unique view of spirituality and in turn, their own view of the teachings.

16 What are the factors, which determine the best kind of connection to the Reiki energy?

There are several factors which determine our alignment with Reiki. Some of the following points play an integral role, whilst other factors contribute, yet have a lesser importance for an effective transmission.

For a good Reiki connection we need to consider the relationship between the teacher and the student.

1. *The teachers' Reiki Lineage.* That they have a sound Reiki lineage, which has the proper methods for passing Reiki onto others.
2. *The teachers' knowledge and ability.* That the teacher has a sound understanding of the Reiki system and the ability to pass this onto others.
3. *The teachers' Reiki transmission.* This represents the teachers Reiki transmission that they received from their teacher.
4. *The teachers' karmic connection to the student.* Meaning is there a good connection, which will enable a solid foundation for learning.
5. *The teachers' karmic path.* How spiritually evolved is the teacher, thereby being a suitable vehicle to benefit others in lasting ways.

Then there are the factors, which affect the student.

1. *The students' karmic connection to the teacher.* Meaning, whether a connection is made where a trust and a ground for learning can endure.
2. *The students' previous karmic path.* This represents the student's ability to learn and understand the teachings.

The more of these factors that come together, the greater potential there is for a student to go deeper into the Reiki system.

17 Is Reiki a form of Channelling?

The term channelling can be confusing as this word has a number of meanings.

Reiki in a sense is a form of channelling, although one should not necessarily consider it to be akin to being a 'Medium' or a form of

'Trance'. In fact the only thing a person requires is the empowerments from a qualified teacher and their own body. When we really take a closer look at how this alignment is created, Reiki is simply the transfer of healing energy from the teacher to the student. The channelling of this energy is the actual transference of Reiki energy. Once the attunements are bestowed to the individual, then one is a Reiki channel.

When someone says that they are a 'Reiki channel', it simply means they have an ability to transmit the Reiki energy through their own body to themselves and others. It does not mean that they can talk to ghosts or distant relatives on the other side.

2

Receiving Reiki

18 Do I have to be ill to receive Reiki?

Reiki is not just for the ill and stricken. Reiki promotes wellness for the body, the emotions and mind. Reiki works on the basis of preventative medicine. Particularly popular in Chinese medicine, this notion being that one need not wait until one is sick before calling the doctor to remedy an illness, rather we see the good doctor when we are well, to promote our bodies sustained health.

To quote Milarepa, one of Tibet's greatest saints: *"When you are strong and healthy, you never think of sickness coming, but it descends with sudden force, like a strike of lightning".*

Keeping these words of wisdom in mind, would we not be better served in our lives if we were to engage in ways, which promote our health and happiness?

Regular Reiki self-treatment will actually enhance the bodies' natural healing rate, as well as reduce lethargy and stress related problems. It comes down to a conscious choice to be well and this begins with actions which support health. As is explained in the teachings, we cause ill health through our misguided thoughts and careless actions, the food and water we consume, the environments we expose ourselves to, and previous karmic activity ripening in this moment.

We can counter illness though a regular self-healing practice. Not waiting until we are ill before we wake up to the fact that we need to cultivate our health on a daily basis.

Regular Reiki self-treatment, as well as our spiritual practice can ensure that many latent diseases of the body can be prevented and purified. When we are treating others we should not just think that if they are well, then no treatment is required. Reiki maintains health, and although our prospective client may exhibit wellness in the present moment, be rest assured that sometime in the future the karmic seeds of previous negative actions will surface and illness will result. It is the nature of being born. All beings are subject to old age, sickness and inevitably, death. Reiki can do much to eradicate much of the karmic influences. The more we give and receive Reiki, the greater potential we have to avert future illness.

When we help others to regain health, we also accumulate merit, which sows future seeds for our own health. Preserving health and pre- serving life, extends our own lives, think of this next time you swat a fly!

Few people ever consider the value of preventative measures when it comes to energy work. We are more than happy to pop a pill or take vitamin supplements; it is only when we really get sick that we think of our health and its importance in our lives.

So Reiki can be a useful tool in maintaining health and long life. It is a tool for your body's health. It is also a tool for your spiritual health.

19 What does one experience during a treatment?

Although not a great deal of importance is placed on experiences during Reiki treatments, (as the nature of phenomena is always in constant flux) it is beneficial to have an understanding of a range of common experiences. This is so we can gain a foundation to understanding some of the ways Reiki translates through our perception.

One way to look at this is through our senses. We experience our world through our eyes, ears, touch and smell.

The following is an overview of experiences common to Reiki in each category.

Visual Perception
In relationship to Reiki our visual mode includes: seeing or perceiving colours, visual imagery, such as - symbols, shapes, swirling patterns, and other imaginary images, as well as dream like images. When these things arise in the mind of the perceiver, this usually indicates material that is being purified from the unconscious mind. It can also be an indication of the particular vibratory level of the energy being

transferred, for example, various colours behind the eyes. It is not overly important to identify what colours correspond to what. This is always in constant motion and simply refers to the transference of healing energy resonating at a particular vibration upon the person receiving it. There is often a tendency to draw upon metaphysical causation or even utilizing colours as a form of diagnosis based on the colours perceived, yet in most cases can be somewhat erroneous and potentially misleading.

Auditory Perception

This takes the form of sound in all its forms, including our internal chatter or inner dialogue. When receiving Reiki, if one is sensitive, one may also experience a heightened increase in sound. Sounds may appear louder and one may experience the sound of the inner workings of the body, such as their own heartbeat, or the flow of blood throughout the body. On an inner level, one may also hear 'inner ear' phenomena. This indicates the sound of the energy flowing through the body.

The most common experience of our auditory perception is that of inner dialogue. This inner dialogue can come in the form of thoughts, or unrelated internal chatter, and this too is a sign of purging unconscious material. In other cases we may receive guidance in the form of messages, words or ideas, springing to mind, such as inspiration or creative solutions to problems. Many creative people often find they have greater clarity in the mind, and more creative ideas, either during or after receiving Reiki.

Kinaesthetic Perception

This is perhaps the most common experience noticed by those who receive Reiki. This includes: the sensation of energy moving through the practitioners' hands to the recipient. This usually expresses itself as warmth or heat through the hands, but sometimes translates as a cool or cold stream of energy as well.

Recipients of a treatment may experience various tingling, pulsing or streaming feelings throughout the body or may even feel as though there is a feeling of hands on the body where the practitioners' hands are not in contact. Other sensations may include a heightened awareness of different areas of the body. Areas may seem to dissolve away or the body may feel like it is levitating or sinking. This illustrates just some of the multitude of experiences, which can arise in ones perception on a kinaesthetic level.

Olfactory Perception

Olfactory Perception describes the sense of smell. This is perhaps one of the least common experiences during a Reiki treatment. Although it is common that one may find that ones sense of smell is more sensitive than usual during and after a Reiki treatment.

Other Olfactory experiences (although not common), may be perceived in conjunction with a past memory. This may include the memory where a particular scent or smell played a part in the past experience.

In summary, ones experiences will vary during a treatment and will often vary each time you receive Reiki. It is best to look at what you experience as a by-product of the transference of Universal Healing energy and not to over identify with your experiences as the goal. If we do become overly concerned with our transitory experiences we can become attached to them and this can become a hindrance to our healing process. If this occurs it can be that our previous experience colours the next, and then we might place an expectation on how our next treatment should be. Ideally it is better to allow a free play of the mind, to arise and fall without attachment, recognising that our experience is a by-product of the minds interplay with Reiki energy.

It is also recommended to write down or journal your Reiki experiences, especially if you are receiving a series of treatments. This is an excellent way to map your progress and see the changes unfolding as you go. Be sure to recognise that whatever you experience is nothing more than a free play of the mind.

Depending upon your ability to perceive subtle energy, this often determines what exactly you experience during a treatment. The following are some of the most frequent experiences related to Reiki.

1. A feeling of heat or warmth in the hands.
2. Tingling or pulsing up or down the arms and in the body.
3. Cold or cool energy running through the hands.
4. The decrease of the mental chatter and an increased calm.
5. A feeling of deep relaxation.
6. Visual impressions, seeing colours, lights or images.
7. Hands feeling drawn to an area.
8. Hands feeling repelled from an area.
9. Hands feeling like they are stuck or glued in an area.

10. Hands feeling like they are a few inches inside the area that is being worked upon.
11. An occasional sharp or dull pain in the hands or arms.
12. A slight vibration in the hands or arms.

20 | How should I feel after a treatment?

Mostly people who experience a Reiki session from an experienced practitioner will generally feel refreshed and energised much like someone who has had a good nights rest. There are also other experiences such as feeling heavy, sleepy, or other disassociated states of consciousness.

If a physical condition has been the priority of the session then one will more often than not, feel sensations surrounding the treatment of the physical ailment, such as a decrease in pain for example. In some cases the body will further purify itself with a clearing of old energies, which can come in many different ways.

Other experiences may be that a person will feel emotional, vulnerable, nurtured, secure, happy, sad, clear, or even sexual, as well as a whole range of different emotions and feelings.

The reason for these experiences, are in direct correlation to the Reiki treatment. Very often the effects of a treatment can continue for hours or days after an initial session. If one uses the analogy of throwing a pebble into a still pond, the ripples make their way out to the whole pond in a gradual fashion. So it is with Reiki. The initial treatment creates waves. This is the experience of the Reiki energy transferring to the recipient. After the session, the effects still continue to ripple out to affect the whole of the person on physical, mental, emotional and spiritual levels.

Depending upon the individual and what is required, the purification process of a treatment may have more or less of an outward appearance. If we think that a pebble is more like a large stone and that the pond has many years of mud at its base, then when the stone is cast, much of the mud (our accumulated conditioning) is stirred up. It then rises to the surface, representing that which requires healing. If we continue to add more fresh water into this pond, the amount of mud will gradually decrease and wash away. This leaves a greater pond, one which is capable of holding good impressions. This illustrates the effects of on-going Reiki treatments. The new water is the Reiki energy and the pond as it grows more and more is ourself with our capacity to share the merits of healing.

21 | Is there anything I should do to support myself after a treatment?

In supporting our healing process, it is best to take timeout after a treatment to integrate the healing energy. Whether this is spending some time in nature, in meditation, or simply being by ourself.

If we have to rush out the door and immediately engage in a stressful environment, one will probably notice the jarring effects of the outer world. This will not have an adverse effect on the treatment, but it would have an unpleasant effect on the person being treated.

Another important point to mention is water. One should drink a moderate amount of water both prior to and after a Reiki treatment. The reason behind this is that Reiki is more conductive if the body is fully hydrated. This will assist the body to release as well as flush out any toxins that have surfaced as a result of the Reiki energy.

22 | Do I need to remove any clothing before a treatment?

Under no circumstances should either the practitioner or recipient remove clothing. Reiki energy has a direct ability to penetrate through clothing, even plaster casts in the case where a broken bone is on the mend. So the need to remove clothing is unnecessary and considering the general application of Reiki, most inappropriate.

It is however, appropriate to assist the recipient in making them as comfortable as possible, so one would recommend that the recipient wear loose comfortable clothing, to remove their shoes and loosen their belt, if wearing one.

When one is facilitating Reiki, the practitioner must pay careful attention to the client's level of comfort and their personal boundaries. One should never place their hands on or near the breasts for women or genitals of a client. It is permissible, however to place one's hands a few inches above these areas as Reiki can be applied both on and above the body with similar results. If a client is uncomfortable even with this, then one must in all cases respect the clients' wishes.

23 Is it normal to experience feeling emotional during or after a Reiki treatment?

Emotions can surface when receiving Reiki. This is part of a purification process on the emotional level. As the purification of the emotional body occurs, deeply held emotions might surface for no apparent reason: anger, frustration, grief, fear, sadness and others. These emotions have most likely been repressed or suppressed from earlier times in our childhood or from prior negative experiences. The Reiki energy has an innate ability to go directly to the cause of peoples problems. Of course, not everyone experiences an emotional release as a result of a Reiki treatment. In most cases one feels deeply at peace and relaxed.

If the energy session brings up emotions, this is an indication that latent emotions are underlying the healing process. One should be reminded that this does not need to be a cathartic and painful experience. Often an emotion will arise in the mind or one will feel their solar plexus and heart stirred with emotion. It is important to know that what ever is coming up is part of your own emotional vibratory matrix being purified. It is not necessary to over identify with these emotions or place blame on others. Our emotions are our own. It is ourself, who experiences them, so how can we blame another?

Sometimes we will be able to identify the emotion and where it comes from and other times not. We may just simply feel sad or down or just very teary for no apparent reason. It is not always necessary to know from where these emotions stem. What we should take out of this is that emotions are present and to acknowledge these as part of a complete healing process.

24 What are some of the ways that I can support myself when emotions arise?

Sometimes by naming the emotion and anchoring it to a place in the body is helpful. So, for example we might say. *"Here is sadness. Sadness resides in my solar plexus"*. Once we have identified the emotion and its location, one can place their hands in this area of the body, giving it healing. Acknowledging this place is an important step to gaining a relationship with the particular emotion arising. From this place we might have a dialogue with this emotion, or write down all the things this emotion brings to mind. This is an *'emptying out'* process. Writing out our emotions or by speaking with others, can bring the underlying emotional issue to the surface. It is then no longer an unidentifiable emotion, but something that can be seen and recognised. This creates further distance and makes space for an alternative perspective.

25 | What are some ways to transform these emotions?

Once we have gained a sense of the emotion, its location and so forth, we can imagine this emotion to be an object of some kind. In this case we state: *"Here is sadness. If this sadness has a shape and looked like something, what would it be?"* Then one imagines this emotion as an object that comes to mind. We observe this object and then begin to disarm the emotion by reducing the objects size or by moving this object away from our self, creating even more distance.

Then one can ask oneself the question: *"If sadness has a remedy, what would this be?"* Then using a positive image, which comes to mind, or a symbolic form, which represents joy or happiness or safety, we imagine this object lodged in the same place as our negative emotion. We then see this symbolic form in the place where the old emotion resided. We build up the experience of this positive symbol and generate its positive qualities more and more.

If you do this process for a while, you'll soon see your sadness is greatly diminished or is completely transformed and gone.

Another way to lessen your emotional purification is to do something nurturing, like taking a bath in sea salts. Taking a long bath with salt is a way of cleansing our emotional body, as well as our whole energy field in general. Put on some gentle music or simply feel into the emotion and sing or tone a sound to express the emotion. Remember, we are not in the business of wallowing in our emotions, rather we desire to acknowledge them, transform them, then move onto better things. Life is too short to get into self-pity. If this is our tendency then we might look at what we get out of this. It is vitally important to examine our emotions as they arise, yet at the same time know that these experiences are transitory. Just in the same way, that clouds form in the sky, then dissolve and move along, so it is with our emotions.

26 When receiving Reiki, why does my body twitch and jolt from time to time?

If one experiences that an area of the body is twitching or experiences a sudden jolt, then these types of experiences usually indicate the de-armouring process. Much of our past and current tensions, including: stress, worry and even negative experiences are stored in our body. These tensions are generally stored in the muscles, vital organs and the fatty deposits of our physical body. When we experience sudden movements, these armoured experiences are surfacing and clearing. So it is a good sign that some of the bodies conditioning is being purified and released. These involuntary movements are also an indication of energy channels (meridians) receiving surges of energy where perhaps the energy flow was insufficient, blocked or depleted.

Another similar experience is where one has the sensation of falling. This can be an indication of an intermediator state or, 'Bardo' (in between state) which is usually experienced between the stages of waking and sleeping. It is not at all uncommon for a person to fall asleep or to have lucid dreams whilst receiving a Reiki treatment. More often than not, this is an indication that the body is in need of deep rest and in many ways this is an indication that the Reiki energy is working at a deep level within the mind.

Many people also report that after receiving a Reiki treatment their first nights sleep is very restful and deep. Other times, people can experience very active and symbolic dreams, again indicating purifications from the person's unconscious mind.

27 Why do the practitioner's hands get hot during treatments?

When we examine the relationship between the outer expression of healing energy and the process of administering Reiki we find the hands will exhibit a change. This is often experienced as warmth or heat in the hands. On the physical level, this interaction between the Reiki energy and the practitioner's physiological manifestations includes some of the following:

A An enhanced blood flow to the periphery of the body. This particularly pertains to increased sensation in the hands, and in some cases, heat in the feet or other parts of the body.

B   An increase and enhancement of neurological activity. This is
    experienced by the brains' electrical impulses slowing down,
    indicating a change in the practitioner's state of consciousness.
C   Other indicators include energetic changes in the body's bio-
    magnetic field, particularly around the hands of the practitioner.
    This also extends to increased activity in the energy centres of the
    head.

The primary reason behind the heat increase in the hands is the
transmission of the Reiki energy as it passes through the practitioner
to the recipient. The energy itself is a higher, more finite vibration. Once
a person has their own vibratory matrix attuned to the Reiki vibration,
this union awakens a pathway for the Reiki energy to travel.

Energy when moving creates heat. This is heightened during
Reiki treatments as a considerably higher volume of vital energy is
transferring. Just in the same way that one could warm ones hands by
rubbing them briskly together, Reiki is an inner movement, without an
outer expression, sending this vibration from one person to another.

28 | Is Reiki always experienced as heat through the hands?

Many Reiki practitioners become concerned that their healing ability has
diminished if heat is not felt during a treatment. The truth of the matter
is Reiki energy can also express itself through the hands as a cool or
cold energy. Whether one senses heat or cool energy, the frequency that
is necessary for the recipient is being transferred. Reiki is an intelligent
energy. Although the experience of cool energy is not as common as
warmth, it is a valid form of energy transference. The intelligence of
Reiki determines the appropriate form for the person receiving the
treatment. In order to accept this point, we must also bring ourselves
back to the awareness that it is not ourselves who are responsible for the
type of healing energy being transferred rather we are simply a conduit
for a higher intelligence acting on behalf of the recipient.

In short, the experience of transferring Reiki healing to another actually has little to do with our own energy or desire for 'this or that' form
of energy. We in effect become a vessel or receiver, much like a radio
sending out a signal. This type of energy being transferred is nothing
personal, just as a radio does not put its own idea into the signal being
transferred, it simply transfers the signal. So it is with Reiki energy.

29 | Why do some people's tummy's rumble during a treatment?

When we are receiving a Reiki treatment it is a common experience for the recipient and sometimes even the practitioners' stomachs to rumble. This sometimes amusing and potentially embarrassing experience is very normal and is due to the body's natural cleansing process. This is activated by the Reiki healing. As the body and mind are transported into a state of consciousness akin to deep sleep, the body simply begins the process that it would normally do whilst one is sleeping. In other cases the treatment is simply aiding an accelerated digestion of food, which has recently been ingested.

Another way to explain this experience is when the body is relaxed. This is part of an unwinding process. The stomach is an area where we hold emotional tension. As a person relaxes more and more, the mind falls deeper into relaxation, then the stomach can release these tensions, which usually manifest as various 'rumbles and gurgles'.

3

The Reiki Styles, Lineage, and History

30 | What is a Reiki lineage and is a lineage in Reiki important?

A Reiki lineage describes the family tree of Reiki teachers and their students, dating back to the founder, Mikao Usui. When we think of a lineage in Reiki we can think a Reiki lineage is much like an ancestry of those who have previously walked the path of Reiki.

To illustrate an example, one well-known Reiki lineage is that of Mrs. Takata. Mrs. Takata was responsible for bringing Reiki to the west for the very first time. Her lineage or family tree goes like this: Usui, Hayashi, and Takata.

To further explain this, Hayashi was a student of Usui. Later Hayashi became a teacher in his own right and in time began to teach his own students. One of his students became Mrs. Takata, who received attunements into Reiki and finally became a teacher in her own right. She in turn began to teach her own students, some of whom became teachers of her system. And so the lineage grows with each generation of teacher.

There are of course many other Reiki lineages, some are many teachers long and some of the methods (*depending upon the teachers in those lineages*) have changed or adapted the Reiki teachings. Subsequently, information may change from teacher to teacher and subsequently the transmission may weaken. On the other hand, there are some Reiki lineages, which have remained unchanged over many decades in Japan, giving students the opportunity to learn a more traditional and original Reiki style.

When a student receives a Reiki attunement, a connection to the lineage of the Reiki teacher is conferred. The students Reiki lineage is in place from that point on. One then usually inherits the teachings and transmission of this lineage with instruction via the teacher.

A Reiki teacher or as is often described, a *'Reiki Master'*, has the ability to give a transmission and to pass on the lineage of their teachers' tradition. Whereas a practitioner can give Reiki to another, yet they cannot pass on the Reiki transmission.

31 Is it possible to have more than one Reiki Lineage?

A teacher or practitioner of Reiki may have more than one Reiki lineage. If one has been initiated into the First Degree by one teacher in one lineage and has received at a later date the Reiki attunement for the Second Degree from another teacher of a different lineage, then effectively this student has two Reiki lineages.

Some teachers have several Reiki lineages, including myself, and have no problem integrating these energies and styles. Although one should never mix up styles, the methods can be passed to others via Reiki attunements with wonderful results.

When we become attuned to Reiki we should first consider the style, the teacher, and their Reiki lineage as all of these points play a key factor in our Reiki development.

Now some people may travel far and wide to gain attunements and teachings from a living teacher who was a student of Mrs. Takata, and indeed there is merit in this. One could think that a Reiki lineage is like a Chinese whisper, the longer the line of teachers, the greater potential for fragmentation and subsequently distortion of the teachings can occur. This notion is largely dependant upon the actual teachers of the lineage and how much or how little they have changed the teachings along the way.

32 What is the difference between traditional and non-traditional Reiki?

Traditional Reiki is considered to be the styles or systems of Reiki which have an uninterrupted line of teachings from the founder, Mikao Usui. Other characteristics include an unbroken lineage of teachers who pass on this tradition in a similar manner, and thirdly, a continuity of practice, methodology and understanding of the material. These points are supportive in determining the style or tradition of Reiki. When a teaching departs from these components, the system changes and either becomes a new system or style and therefore becomes a new Reiki lineage. A simple example of this is Hayashi's style of Reiki. Hayashi was one of Usui's students. Hayashi learnt several methods from Usui and received some of the transmissions for his teachings. However, shortly after Usui's death, Hayashi took it upon himself to make significant changes to Usui's system. So much so, that only a few parts of Usui's practice remained. Hayashi in turn, introduced his own form of attunements and hands-on procedures. In the west, many Reiki teachers consider Hayashi to be a teacher of the Usui System of Natural Healing. Although Hayashi learnt from Usui, his system was changed to the degree that his new style bore little resemblance to his teacher's style of Reiki. Therefore, although Hayashi bears a Reiki lineage to Usui, his Reiki style is considerably different. Once the methodology and the attunement procedures of a system change, they are no longer the same. It is most important to make clear distinctions where changes are made within a system.

One should be aware that the majority of the Reiki styles available today have already been combined with other systems of healing and religion. In other cases they have been invented or created out of various teachers' insights, as well as channelled material alike.

33 | What are the main Reiki lineages available today?

There are many forms or styles of Reiki today. The following is a list of some of the more popular Reiki styles as well as many new and invented systems which are listed on the internet. Although some of the non-traditional styles are diversely different to traditional Reiki, it is up to the individual to investigate the style which feels best for them.

The following is an A to Z guide to the various Reiki styles.

1. Adama Starfire Reiki
2. Alef Reiki
3. Amanohuna Reiki
4. Angelic Raykey
5. Angel Touch Reiki
6. Anugraha Reiki
7. Ascension Reiki
8. Authentic Reiki

9. Blue Star Reiki
10. Brahma Satya Reiki
11. Buddho Ennersense Reiki
12. Dragon Reiki
13. Dorje Reiki
14. Fusion Reiki
15. Gakkai Reiki
16. Gendai Reiki
17. Golden Age Reiki
18. Ichi Sekai Reiki
19. Imara Reiki
20. Innersun Reiki
21. Japanese Reiki
22. Jikiden Reiki
23. Jinlap Maitre Reiki
24. Johrei Reiki
25. Kava Reiki
26. Karuna Ki
27. Karuna Reiki
28. Ken Reiki-do
29. Kundalini Reiki
30. Lightarian Reiki
31. Magnussa Phoenix Reiki
32. Mari El
33. Medicine Buddha Reiki (Sangye Menlha Reiki)
34. Medicine Dharma Reiki (Men Chhos Reiki)
35. Medicine Reiki
36. Monastic Seven Degree Reiki
37. New Life Reiki
38. Ni Kawa Reiki
39. Osho Neo Reiki
40. Radiance Technique
41. Rainbow Reiki
42. Raku Reiki
43. Reiki Jin Kei Do
44. Reiki Plus
45. Rei Ki Tummo
46. Sacred Path Reiki
47. Sai baba Reiki
48. Saku Reiki
49. Satya Japanese Reiki
50. Shakyamuni Reiki
51. Siddhearta Reiki
52. Silverwolf Reiki
53. Seichim or Seichem
54. Sun Li Chung Reiki
55. Tanaki Reiki
56. Tera-Mai and Tera-Mai Seichim
57. Tibetan Soul Star Reiki
58. Tibetan Reiki
59. Universal Reiki Dharma
60. Usui-Do
61. Usui Reiki Ryoho
62. Usui Shiki Ryoho
63. Usui Teate Reiki
64. Usui/Tibetan Reiki
65. Usui Universal Healing Reiki
66. Vajra Reiki
67. Violet Flame Reiki
68. Wei Chi Tibetan Reiki

34 How old is Reiki and from where did it originate?

Many sources only have approximate dates, ranging somewhere between the tail end of the 19th Century and the early 20th Century. Other sources in Japan claim that formal teaching of Reiki officially began in

1920, whilst others still, state it began in 1918. More recent channeled information claims a much longer history, dating back some 2550 years to the historical Buddha.

If one investigates the healing practices within the traditions of Tibetan Buddhism, one finds similar references to the teachings of Mikao Usui. Healing practices have been a part of almost every religion and culture throughout time. It is no wonder than similar ideas and views about healing abound.

Perhaps the full story concerning Reiki's roots will never be truly known, however what matters most are the teachings and how these can benefit others.

35 | Who founded Reiki?

The founder of Reiki was a Japanese Buddhist man named Mikao Usui.

Mikao Usui was born in the village of Taniai, which is now called Miyama cho, in the Gifu Prefecture on August 15, 1865, where his ancestors had lived for eleven generations. His ancestry dates back to the *Chiba clan who were once an influential samurai family in Japan. His family also belonged to the Tendai sect of Buddhism and when he was four, he was sent to a Tendai Monastery to receive his primary education.

Mikao Usui was born into a class system and therefore received a privileged education. When he was 12 years of age Mikao began martial arts training. He studied two martial arts called 'Aiki Jutsu' and 'Yagyu Ryu' and attained a high level of proficiency in weaponry and grappling. He spoke many languages and became well-versed in medicine, theology and philosophy. Usui's memorial states that from his youth he had surpassed his fellow students and that he was well versed in history, medicine, Buddhist and Christian scriptures, and Waka poetry. It also states on Usui's memorial that Usui was versed in divination, incantation, and physiognomy and like many intellectuals of his day was also fascinated with the 'new science' coming from the West.

Throughout Usui's early adulthood, he lived in Kyoto with his wife, Sadako Suzuki, and two children, a son named Fuji and a daughter named Toshiko.

It is believed that during this time, Usui began to take a deeper interest in meditation. He furthered his studies and undertook protracted retreats to further his spiritual development. Some sources indicate Usui took formal training in Shingon Buddhism. He is also believed to have undertaken the position of a lay Tendai priest (Zaike) and is said to have taken the Buddhist name of Gyoho.

Mikao Usui spent much time and money pursuing his new-found spiritual path by studying and collecting Buddhist scriptures. In particular, he studied Buddhist healing techniques and invested an enormous amount of money collecting old medical texts.

Kyoto was home to many large and extensive Buddhist libraries and monasteries that had collections of ancient texts. Usui did much of his research there. For many years, Usui continued to collect, study, and practice these medical texts. He became an advanced practitioner and master of meditation.

Over time, Usui became a respected and learned Buddhist teacher with a following of devoted students. They met regularly and Usui would teach from the texts that he had been collecting. The focus of his teachings was on healing and benefiting humankind through healing

Crest of the Chiba clan of Usui's ancestors

The Usui Memorial

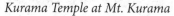

Kurama Temple at Mt. Kurama   *View from Mt. Kurama*

practice. They practiced elaborate rituals for averting newly created diseases that were ravaging Japan, as well as esoteric practices for healing every type of illness.

It is unclear when Mikao Usui actually began taking on students. The Usui memorial states that he did not begin teaching his system of healing until 1922. However, other sources state that he began teaching long before. For example, Mariko Suzuki, the cousin of Mikao Usui's wife was said to have begun training with Usui in 1915. Other sources state that Usui's system of healing began as early as the late 1890s. Whether this teaching took the form of meditation or his system of hands-on healing, is not certain.

According to the Usui Memorial, one day he decided to commence an intensive meditation retreat on Mt. Kurama. It is not known how long he spent in meditation however some accounts suggest it was 21 days. During this time Usui fasted and undertook a practice called Kushu Shinren, which is a type of meditation practice. At the completion of his time on Mt. Kurama he gained a realization into the way of healing. According to several sources including his memorial stone, a great energy appeared over his head and he received the empowerment of the Universal healing energy. Through his prior learning and spiritual attainment he formulated a system of healing which later became known as Reiki.

After much contemplation and careful consideration he decided to share these teachings with others. Usui first practiced his newly discovered method on his family and friends. Then he began to offer his healing method to the lower class district of Kyoto. Kyoto is a religious centre and the people in the streets are taken in and cared for with each family looking out for its own. Usui opened his home to many and for seven years he brought Reiki to them. This gave him the opportunity to perfect and refine his new healing method. Meanwhile, he continued to hold regular classes for his growing 'circle' of Buddhist followers, and further developed and refined his system.

It seems from recent research that Usui taught his system in different ways depending upon his student's level of understanding and ability. His earlier teachings were less formalized. Some teachings introduced the use of mantra and symbol, whilst others utilized methods of meditation. Irrespective of the methods used, the vehicle was the practice of healing.

In April of the 11th year of Taisho (1922), Usui moved to Tokyo where he worked as the secretary to Pei Gotoushin, the Prime Minister of Tokyo. He opened a Reiki clinic in Harajuku, Aoyama, outside Tokyo and began to set up classes and teach his system of Reiki. Some sources suggest this was the formation of the Reiki Gakkai and purportedly, many students came to study.

It is said that Usui taught Reiki to just over 2000 people and out of these students some sources say he trained 21 students to the teachers level (Shinpiden).

In 1922, Usui reportedly founded a Reiki society, called the Usui Reiki Ryoho Gakkai, and acted as its first president. This society was open to those who had studied Usui's Reiki. This society still exists today and there have been six presidents since Usui:

Mr. Juzaburo Ushida 1865-1935,
Mr. Kanichi Taketomi 1878-1960,
Mr. Yoshiharu Watanabe (unknown – 1960),
Mr. Hoichi Wanami 1883-1975,
Ms. Kimiko Koyama 1906-1999;
Mr. Masayoshi Kondo (current president)

On September 1, 1923 the devastating Kanto earthquake struck Tokyo and surrounding areas. Most of the central part of Tokyo was leveled and totally destroyed by fire. Over 140,000 people were killed. In response to this catastrophe, Usui and his students offered Reiki to countless victims. His clinic soon became too small to handle the throng of patients, so in February of 1924, he built a new clinic in Nakano, outside Tokyo. His fame spread quickly all over Japan and he began receiving invitations from all over the country to come and teach his healing methods. Usui was awarded a Kun San To from the Emperor, which is a very high award (much like an honorary doctorate), given to those who have done honourable work. His fame soon spread throughout the region and many prominent healers and physicians began requesting teachings from him.

Usui quickly became very busy as requests for teachings of Reiki continued to grow. He traveled throughout Japan (not an easy undertaking in those days), to teach and give Reiki empowerments. This started to take its toll on his health and he began experiencing mini-strokes from stress. Usui then left for a teaching tour in the Western part of Japan. Finally, on March 9, 1926, while in Fukuyama, Usui died of a fatal stroke. He was 62 years old.

Usui's body was cremated and his ashes were placed in a temple in Tokyo. Shortly after his death, students from the Reiki society in Tokyo erected a memorial stone at Saihoji Temple in the Toyatama district in Tokyo. According to the inscription on his memorial stone, Usui taught Reiki to over 2,000 people. Many of these students began their own clinics and founded Reiki schools and societies. By the 1940s there were about 40 Reiki schools spread all over Japan. Most of these schools taught the method of Reiki that Usui had developed.

36 | Do any of Usui's original manuscripts remain intact today?

As more and more information about the life and teachings of Mikao Usui emerge, we are finding how this historical jigsaw puzzle fits together. Since 1993, when the first details concerning Usui's manual appeared, via a German Reiki Master, Frank Arjava Petter, some of Usui's original teachings were revealed and later published.

Some of these findings include: The Usui Hikkei, (practitioner manual); the Memorial at Usui's grave, (erected by members of his Reiki society); as well as stories and information from students of Mikao Usui. It is unclear whether all that there is to know about Usui has been revealed to date and no doubt, further revelations concerning the Usui system of Reiki will continue to be expounded in the years to come.

37 | Was Mikao Usui a Christian or a Buddhist?

The confusion of this point is due to the misinformation that Mrs. Takata generated about the life and times of Usui. In Mrs. Takata's historical account of Usui, she describes Usui as a Christian. In fact as a result of her influence, many teachers around the world still propagate this story. One will even find in almost every Reiki book, particularly those published before 1993, opening paragraphs often describing Usui as being a Christian Minister at Doshisha University. Mrs. Takata also said that Usui was said to have gained his Doctorate at the University of Chicago, yet both of these alleged claims were subsequently proven to be false. Following on from this question, one could speculate that Mrs. Takata was simply conveying information about Usui from her teacher, Hayashi, who is said to have been a Methodist Christian.

On the other hand, we could say that Mrs. Takata adjusted the known Reiki history to make Reiki more widely accepted in America. Particularly after Japans involvement in the Second World War and with the bombing of Pearl Harbour, Mrs. Takata more than likely used her inventiveness to amend the history to make the origins of Usui and his system of Reiki more palatable for the somewhat conservative (mostly Christian) Americans of her day.

4

Before learning Reiki

38 How do I find a suitable Reiki teacher?

Finding a Reiki teacher is sometimes a synchronistic experience, and sometimes it can be a rather confusing process. Because there are so many different types of Reiki, Reiki teachers, and opinions, it can be hard to know where to start. The following eight points are part of a number of general questions you should ask a teacher of Reiki when browsing the New Age supermarket. If you cover these questions you will generally be able to determine their level of proficiency and whether they know enough to teach you.

Point 1. Ask which style of Reiki they teach. Many teachers will say they teach 'Usui Reiki' however this generally means the Takata or Western Reiki tradition. Check the teacher's lineage in Reiki. They should be able to tell you who they learnt from and their Reiki Lineage dating back to the founding teacher, Usui. If they cannot do this, be wary. Some Reiki lineages have long legs and as a result, may be watered down significantly or even worse, distorted by wrong views and insufficient training from previous instructors. It is not only a matter of getting *'your monies worth'* it is also about finding a spiritually sound teacher who you can place your trust in.

Point 2. Ask how long the teacher has been teaching and how long was their own teacher training. If they learnt all three Reiki levels in one weekend and just started teaching the following weekend, then this should raise your alarm bells.

Determine whether they teach regularly and whether they use Reiki on themselves and others on a regular basis.

Point 3. Check to see what you will be learning and the length of time it will take to learn each level. Also ask if there will be time to practice the methods. Most classes take at least 14 hours to teach. Ask whether your teacher offers ongoing practice times or ongoing support after the class.

Point 4. How much money will your training cost. Be wary of extremely high fees and also of suspiciously low fees. Ask the teacher what they charge, why they charge the amount and what will you receive for your investment.

Point 5. Will you receive a training manual and will you be issued with a Reiki Certificate. Ask How does one qualify for the Certificate and does the teacher offer an accreditation process.

Point 6. Determine whether you are able to take notes in the class or record the information presented.

Point 7. Does your prospective teacher 'walk their talk?' Do they seem authentic and genuine by nature? If you feel like you wouldn't buy a used car from this person, you may wish to reconsider investing your spiritual development with them. When all is said and done in the end you need to trust your gut instinct.

Point 8. Speak to other students who have learnt with this teacher, they will be able to give you a perspective on the classes on offer.

39   Can one learn Reiki online or solely from books?

When we look at Reiki we can split the teachings into two parts. The first being information and the second being transmission.

Information is the nuts and bolts of the system, these are the sorts of things which can be learnt from a book or online, provided the methods that are given generate results and come from a genuine source. If this is the case, then this is an effective and acceptable way to learn where one might not otherwise be able to study, due to distances and so forth.

The other and essential side to Reiki is that of transmission. This transmission comes to the student in the form of a teacher who bestows the Reiki attunements. It is these attunements that align the student with the Reiki ability. This part cannot be transmitted through a book or website. One requires a living teacher to give this transmission. Information has its place, but transmission is the foundation of the system and is most essential.

Now one can learn Reiki at a distance and many Reiki teachers now offer Reiki training over the Internet. A teacher can give the student the Reiki attunements at a distance and if done correctly will effect a transmission of the Reiki ability in that student. However, nothing beats a direct transmission and the feeling that comes from learning Reiki in a class setting. Here, one has the opportunity to grow and share with others under the direct instruction and guidance of a qualified teacher. If, due to difficult circumstances one is prevented from travel or has a disability which might prevent learning Reiki in a class setting, then distant attunements may be an option worthy of consideration. This type of distant learning does require ongoing interaction between the student and teacher, so it is most important to be sure that the teacher has the capacity to be there for your on-going support and development.

40 | Are psychic abilities a part of Reiki?

For one to learn Reiki, clairvoyant or psychic ability is not a requirement, nor should one place a tremendous amount of importance on these kinds of experiences. As one gradually progresses through the Reiki system, inner abilities often begin to emerge for some practitioners and this is due to the strengthened relationship with the Reiki energy. Many practices of the original Reiki system actually support the opening of ones inner perception, such as methods to directly perceive areas of imbalance. As these abilities emerge, one can use these methods as ways to consciously and more accurately involve oneself in the healing process.

On the flipside, one can be drawn into self-deception if one places too much importance on 'all things Psychic'. Here one can overly read into everything. One begins to receive *'messages from the other side'*. One begins to give vague readings during treatments and suddenly, Reiki becomes a Psychic reading and all the intelligent people run away.

Unless one has done a lot of inner work, one can tend to operate out of ones' own projections, perceiving these to be real. One is cautioned to remember that one is working in partnership with the Reiki energy and not ones Ego.

It is not much use having inner abilities to impress others or to boost ones ego into thinking it has an 'all-seeing power'. I have personally seen many people become deluded by awakening these inner abilities then fool themselves into thinking that these abilities are an end in themself. Psychic ability can be a bi-product of ongoing Reiki practice, but it is not the goal. If one can clearly use these abilities for healing with a humble disposition then this is wonderful, just so long as one remembers the view that inner abilities are a way to skilfully benefit others.

41 What should I do to prepare myself before taking a Reiki class?

It is useful to make some preparations before taking a Reiki class. Where possible, avoid the following: stressful or emotionally charged situations, negative people and environments, late nights, violent movies or negative conversations. The overuse of recreational drugs, alcohol, and stimulants such as caffeine or foods, can have a counter effect as these substances many not suit your natural disposition.

Increase the following: Peaceful situations, take time out for your self for reflection and meditation. Get lots of rest and be self-nurturing. Some light exercise, or other pleasurable activities can benefit as well as writing in your journal, setting goals and thinking positive thoughts.

Some other preparations might include the following:

Clean up your clutter. Have a Garage Sale, give gifts to friends, offer prayers for friends and loved ones to be well and happy. Sing, stretch, laugh, relax and play. Do what makes you feel good. These are the sorts of things to embrace prior to learning Reiki.

Don't be concerned if your life prevents this, as obstacles are usually an indication of pre-workshop purification. Just do the best you can and most importantly, relax.

42 If I feel heat in my hands, without the Reiki attunements, does this mean that I have Reiki or is this some other form of energy?

It may be that what you are experiencing is an expression of healing energy however there are many kinds of healing energy, even noticeable from one Reiki style to the next. One can think of it like a multi-faceted crystal. Each facet is unique, yet it is part of the whole. When one focuses light through the crystal, light reflects in each facet. So with each form of healing energy, comes a unique flow of energy. Some people are naturally attuned to Reiki; whilst others are attuned to other healing energies. Although people sometimes feel energies moving through their hands during massage, lovemaking or other 'hands-on' activities, it does not necessarily mean that it is Reiki energy. For the most part, one experiences one's own vital energy.

When it comes to healing work, a common experience for those who have not received the attunements is that the practitioner becomes rather drained or depleted. The reason for this is that they are using their own life-force energy during the session. This is of course, rarely the case with Reiki.

The Reiki attunements are designed to give you a direct connection to an unlimited source of healing energy, which is always there when you need it.

One could think that at times, those who are naturally in tune with this ability have an antenna picking up the radio station, Reiki. But due to various calamities and the conditioning of daily life, the signal drops out from time to time. At other times when we really want this healing ability to work, it seems to vanish, then at other times when we are not expecting a connection, all of a sudden, it manifests. So, the general experience is that our antenna is not so reliable and is subject to fluctuations. What the Reiki attunements do is create an alignment, which is always in tune.

These transmissions make the energy a reliable source, which we can depend upon and will be there every time we place hands-on.

We must also remember that Reiki is a unique method and although many other healing systems abound, Reiki energy has a unique quality and practice. If one uses this system and has received the attunements by a qualified teacher, then there is a noticeable difference before and after the attunement.

43 | Is Reiki just for the gifted or can anyone learn?

Anyone can utilize the methods of Usui's Reiki system. Learning Reiki is by no means limited to anyone and one does not require any prior ability to learn. The system of aligning a person to this ability is Universal in nature, so a person need only have an energy system, (which everyone has) to have this ability activated. If the teacher has a correct system of attunement, and if they know how to give attunements to others, then in most cases people will achieve the desired result.

Over the last 12 years, I have personally initiated over 1,500 people into Reiki and there has not been one person who has not achieved the results. I have also re-attuned many people who had previously attended a Reiki workshop with another teacher, yet they had no discernable connection. This only leads me to believe that there must be many Reiki Masters who are missing the necessary keys of the attunements to make the necessary alignments. Therefore, one must closely examine one's teacher to determine their suitability.

44 | Are some people better at doing Reiki than others?

Although everyone can do Reiki, it seems that some students excel in the higher Reiki levels more so than others. Just like there are those people who are artistic or those who have 'an ear' for music. Some people can play an excellent tune with feeling, yet cannot read music, whilst others can play a piece of music with precise technical ability, yet cannot express the emotional quality of the music.

By this I mean that some students have a more refined inner ability. Even if a music student practices for hours each day, they will develop an excellent tune, there are those students however, who upon hearing the music once, can play it with ease and do not require many hours of practice to accomplish this same level of expertise.

What is the reason behind this? It comes down to the accumulated storehouse of merit from one's former lives or previous karma. A merit storehouse represents all of our positive actions from former lives. Some people simply have a greater capacity for good. Based on our previous virtuous actions in former lives we come into this life with a 'karmic' head start. Just as there are people who are really good at art, there are also people who are really good at healing work. Some people accumulate a small merit storehouse and others accumulate a greater storehouse. The greater accumulated merit, the greater capacity one has to benefit others.

We have every opportunity to progress and to better ourselves. In this very life we can purify countless lifetimes of negativity, but it does require work. One way to clear karmic debts is through generosity and service to others. Service is the quick path, as we learn to benefit all beings, life gets easier and we begin to see the unfortunate circumstances in our lives as purifications and therefore strengthen our resolve to continue working for the greater good.

As this is purified more and more, we tend to take things less personally. We see others doing harmful actions against us and realise they are operating out of their own suffering and confusion. Through this view we create space to see things as they really are. In this way we are no longer the target of others. We learn to create more and more circumstances, which will further our path and spend our time with those who support us on the way. This is a sure way to progress along the Reiki path.

45 Will Reiki work on someone who is not receptive to it?

One does not need to believe in Reiki for it to work. Very rarely will you encounter someone who does not notice the benefits of a Reiki treatment. Provided the practitioner has received the Reiki attunements and knows how to apply the methods, with ongoing treatments, benefits (in all but a few cases), will result.

For people who are new to Reiki, I usually encourage a healthy sense of scepticism as this affords people to trust in their own experience. It is important to use one's discriminating wisdom. Blind faith alone can move mountains, but direct experience cultivates understanding and a broad perspective. You have to check things out for yourself. Sometimes you will encounter a sceptic who would rather theorise for hours about the possible effects of Reiki, without taking the step of actually receiving a Reiki treatment. It is like trying to describe to someone from another planet what ice cream tastes like. We could use all kinds of descriptions to explain the experience, but we would not be able to give that person the reality of it. If someone asks me, *"what does Reiki feel like"*, in most cases I will say: *"lie down and I'll show you"*. Just in the same way that you would be better off buying your alien friend an ice cream and saying: *"here, try it yourself"*.

46 Which types of abilities will I have after learning the First Degree in Reiki?

The beginner's level or First Degree Reiki focuses on how to heal oneself and others. Essentially this is what is transferred with the Reiki First Degree attunements. The attunements are usually given in 4 separate stages or in some traditions given as one attunement. During a First Degree class, one will usually learn a series of hand placement positions for treating oneself and others, as well as learning the Reiki Principles, the Reiki History and some procedures for centring oneself. Traditionally, the first level is instructed either as a weekend intensive or gradually over a number of weekly meetings. After this training period the student has a direct ability to transfer healing energy to oneself in the form of self-treatments and the ability to give others Reiki healing. Once these energy alignments are given to the student via the teacher, this ability continues from that day forth and activates whenever one places their hands on any living thing.

Depending on which particular style of Reiki you learn, other practices may be given. These might include the use of symbols, distant healing methods and spiritual practices which assist in enhancing energy flow. These practices are usually given at the Second Degree. One may also learn how to establish personal boundaries, how to bless objects as well as how to clear old energy from rooms. Other techniques may include, how to work intuitively with Reiki, scanning the aura, reading the aura as well as many other methods and meditations to name but a few.

47 How long does a Reiki treatment last?

The length of time required during a treatment is largely dependant upon the person being treated. If someone has a terminal disease, they may require hours of Reiki, whilst a small child may only need 15 minutes. It also depends on how many people are administering the treatment at one time. If more than one person is giving another Reiki, then one can say that the treatment time is halved.

In some Reiki circles, a full treatment which treats the head, trunk of the body, legs, shoulders, and back may take up to one and a half hours, whilst other schools recommend half hour treatments. This is only a general guide and as one becomes more adept at treating others, a subtle ability to perceive when enough Reiki has been administered becomes apparent.

With Reiki, the body takes what it needs. We could use the analogy of the body being a dry sponge and the Reiki energy being water. Once the sponge has absorbed, as much water is it can hold, then no more water is required. If one is giving regular Reiki treatments to another, for example once daily, the treatment time may also begin to decrease. There is no hard and fast rule here and one needs to determine what is necessary for each person individually. We all have different needs and so the amount required from person to person varies.

5

Reiki and its effects

48 Can someone who is physically disabled learn Reiki?

Yes, but how one learns is really dependent upon the disability. As Reiki is mostly administered through the hands, if one hand is missing for example or both hands, then a teacher can attune the pathways of energy in the feet. I once taught a student who was missing a hand due to a motor vehicle accident. In this case the remaining hand was attuned and the individual was able to give treatments in much the same way as anyone else. Reiki also can be administered via the eyes; through certain energy centres as well as through the breath. Some Reiki styles focus a great deal of emphasis on the mind, so the possibilities for learning are considerable. In the event that the person has another disability that prevents the use of all limbs, then distant healing methods can be given.

49 Can someone who is mentally disabled learn Reiki?

It would depend upon the individual's mental disability to the degree of which form of treatment is being used. If the person has Downs Syndrome then the way Reiki is taught and explained is somewhat simplified. So long as ones mental faculties are intact and one has some control of the body, then one can usually learn the basic healing methods. If the person has no mental control, the Reiki attunements can still be given at a distance or in person and acts as a blessing for the person.

Preferably, receiving regular Reiki treatments is beneficial. As an alternative, if one has a carer, the carer could learn and integrate the use of hands-on healing with the person's daily activities.

50 Can someone learn Reiki who is suffering from a Mental illness?

In the case where a person is suffering from a mental illness one can still learn, however careful consideration needs to be placed on making the experience as grounded as possible. We also need to consider what mental illness is. What is the severity of the condition and is the individual being assisted with the appropriate intervention of a Therapist, Phycologist or Physician. In such cases one needs to familiarise oneself with the condition and make suitable arrangements as well as taking the advice given by these qualified health professionals.

If someone wishes to learn Reiki in this condition, it is not worth the risk if the person concerned has lost touch with reality and could create a whole new set of delusions surrounding the practice and effects of Reiki. For treatment, it is advisable that the individual remains grounded and present. As Reiki has a tendency to alter ones consciousness, a person who spends a great deal of time in altered states would benefit by remaining close to mundane matters. Here one would talk to the person and keep their attention on something other than the treatment being administered. In all cases, check with a professional in this area before proceeding.

51 Does Reiki work every time?

Provided the practitioner is using Reiki energy and they have been properly trained then one can be assured that some benefit will be derived from a treatment. In the case when Reiki seemingly does not have an effect, it can be that one may benefit from accumulated sessions. Here with ongoing treatments, positive effects will generally manifest themselves. Reiki goes to the area of imbalance most in need. Cases where no change has been indicated can be based upon the recipient's level of awareness or ability to sense subtle energy in the body. If one is heavily armoured and emotionally cut off, then it may take several treatments to release these tensions. The healing effects may also have a delayed effect in the body. One may not feel the effects of a treatment until two to three days later.

52 | Why can't everyone just do Reiki without formal instruction?

The problem we face is that we have forgotten the way. Through our conditioned mind and karmic past we have become out of tune with the Universal flow. The Reiki attunements are a specific way to awaken or tune in this ability. If you don't have the methods, this alignment is difficult to effect. We need someone who has those methods to re-attune our vibratory matrix to match the same vibratory matrix of Reiki. If it was simply a matter of 'will', then we would not require the Reiki attunements. The reality is that Reiki is a specific method and being so, requires specific instruction and transmission for the ability to work.

In the same way that if you get enough Monkeys with enough typewriters, you will eventually write the complete works of Shakespeare, the intelligence of Mind always finds a way. The attunements, however, speed up the process, and with this we create the pathway to healing that works every time.

53 | How many treatments does a person require before they are healed?

To determine how many Reiki treatments one requires before one is healed is dependant upon a number of factors.

The first is the type and severity of illness or imbalance. The second is the origin or karmic cause of the illness, and the third is the method which is being used to counter the illness. These are the factors determining wellness.

Unfortunately, there is no one answer to this question as so many variables come into play. Each person will heal at a varying rate depending on the strength of his or her constitution. No two illnesses are the same, just the same as no two people are the same. In general, Reiki will heal most people. It then becomes a question of time. There is also a big difference between being healed and being cured. It is best to approach healing work with this in mind and to do ones best to administer Reiki so that it might heal not only the symptoms exhibited by the recipient but the cause as well.

54 | How do drugs and alcohol affect the Reiki energy?

As a general rule the use of recreational drugs and alcohol do not mix with Reiki. In all but a few exceptions to the rule, a Reiki practitioner should not treat another if under the influence of these substances. Although Reiki energy will flow when the practitioner is under the effects of drugs and alcohol, this should not be an excuse for general practice.

The only exception being is in the case of an emergency. For example, I was once at a party where someone had injured themselves. Although, previously I had had a few drinks and was feeling more than jovial, none the less, the person needed immediate assistance. While someone else was calling an ambulance, I was attending to the injury with first aid as well as incorporating Reiki into the treatment of the injury.

When we are receiving a Reiki treatment we are inviting the purest form of divine energy into our body and mind to affect our healing. The experience of Reiki is oftentimes a very peaceful and even transcendental experience, let alone having to distort this with the use of drugs and other substances.

On an energetic level, the use of many drugs has an adverse affect on the human energy field. Many drugs dissipate ones personal boundaries, leaving the energy field open to psychic transference and psychic invasion of lower energies.

Now I am not personally against the moderate use of recreational drugs, if people wish to explore these substances this is their choice. The point is that these substances should not be mixed with Reiki.

55 | Is a group Reiki treatment better that one person giving a treatment?

If one has the opportunity to experience a Reiki treatment from many Reiki practitioners then this is a wonderful thing. It would not be fair to say that receiving Reiki from a group of practitioners is better than one, it is just different. Certainly additional practitioners lessen the time that is required to complete the healing. The difference might be illustrated as a glass vessel being filled with pure clear water. If one person is administering a treatment to another, then this is like one stream of water into the vessel. With one stream, it will take longer to fill. If we add two, three, five or ten streams of water, then in no time at all we will achieve a full vessel. Reiki in a group setting acts in a similar fashion. Many hands make light work when treating others with Reiki.

One story, which illustrates the effects of how many practitioners can generate effective healing, comes from a woman in the United States who we will call Mrs. M.

Mrs. M had been diagnosed with terminal cancer 12 months previously. After repeated chemotherapy and months of operations with little sign of improvement, Mrs. M's life was in serious contention. Her surgeon had given her a life expectancy of 3 months at best.

Determined to fight her illness, she undertook regular Reiki treatments and during this time heard about the benefits of Reiki absent healing.

Armed with the Internet, she contacted 1000s of Reiki practitioners and Reiki masters from all around the world, asking for them to send her distant healing. In a short span of time her general health improved and she was well on the road to recovery. Out of these 1,000s of healers, something must have worked because when she was tested some months later, no sign of her cancer remained. Her doctor and surgeon were naturally scratching their heads and demanded she be re-tested. Yet after repeated tests, no sign of the cancer remained. To my knowledge, some 6 years later, Mrs. M is still fighting fit and has had no relapse of illness whatsoever.

56 | How many treatments can a Reiki practitioner give before they become drained of their life force energy?

A common misunderstanding is that Reiki healing is given by utilising ones own life-force energy. If Reiki was dependant on this, we could think of our own capacity as healers to be considerably limited. Much like having a limited amount of funds in the bank, each time we give a healing we would be drawing on these funds. Eventually they would run out and we would be in serious debt, or in this case depleted. The system of Reiki acts in a unique fashion. The healing energy of Reiki comes through the practitioner. Much like filling a vessel, once the energy has filled the practitioner, it overflows into the recipient, boosting their own life force energy. The practitioner is simply a conduit or vehicle for transmitting the healing energy.

Where some other systems of healing utilize their own life force energy and can be subject to depletion, Reiki does not fall into this category.

57 Is Reiki always facilitated with the hands above the body or on the body?

It's both. Reiki can be applied to a person with the hands on, hands off or a combination of the two. Many of the ways that Reiki is practiced in the west is with the hands placed upon the body. In some countries unless you are a licensed physiotherapist, a Doctor or Reverend, you are not permitted to place the hands on at all. Practitioners in these counties get around this by placing their hands slightly above the body, transferring healing energy through the recipients energy field. The effect is much the same.

When treating others, it is usually considered the 'norm' to place the hands on the areas of injury or imbalances, treating the area of concern directly. In the event that the injury is too painful to touch or the person's area of imbalance is located in a private area, then the hands placed directly above is an effective alternative. Much healing is communicated in a nurturing way by the hands being placed upon the body. Touch communicates care and love. Touch heals, just ask any Mother.

In other Reiki styles, specific methods utilize the transference of healing energy above the body to balance and purify imbalances within the energy field of the recipient. There are other styles again which utilize a combination of hands on and hands above.

The Reiki energy will active above the body, though generally the experience felt by the recipient in these cases is felt to a lesser degree as no physical contact is being made.

Many Reiki practitioners use a combination of these methods and this way the cause and symptoms can be treated in a conscious manner through the practitioners healing abilities.

6

First Degree Reiki

58 | How important is faith and intent when giving Reiki?

This is one of those questions, which has two answers. For Reiki to have benefit it does not require the recipient or the practitioner to believe in it for healing to occur. Once attuned, the energy simply flows and whether the mind of the practitioner is focussed on the transference of this healing energy, or if the recipient is doubtful that Reiki will have any benefit, this seems to have little effect on the positive transmission of healing. On the other hand, if one has faith in the process and if the practitioner has a focused intention for healing, there seems to be greater results and experiences with the outcome. With a willing openness and faith in healing, unfolds another level, which is the power of the mind.

It has been well documented throughout all major healing systems and religions of belief and experience alike that the power of intention can do much to heal. Sages of old have said this time and again. The Buddha said: *"We are what we think, with our thoughts we create the world"*, Pythagoras said: *"You must think as you would become"*, Jesus said: *"The Kingdom of God lies within you"*. With each thought we create our world. Through prayer, we create, we manifest, and we become. Although Reiki does not require these devices, nonetheless they have tremendous power and knowing this, we should use the best of both worlds. One should never underestimate the power of the mind.

There are those who contend that Reiki is only a placebo and although I know this to be a fallacy, the important thing to remember is whether healing occurs, and if so, isn't this what is most important at the end of the day?

Reiki is not akin to Faith healing or Spiritual healing, yet faith and trust in one's healing process and trust in the divine intelligence of Reiki can certainly aid our process.

An old story which illustrates the power of faith comes from the Buddha-Dharma. It goes something like this.

An old Tibetan woman who practiced the teachings of Buddha had a son who was a travelling merchant. Being a merchant, he frequently visited India for business. One day his mother said to him, "India is the Buddha's country. Please, be so kind as to bring me some relic of the Buddha's land that might inspire my devotion to the teachings."

The son left, but consumed with his business activities, completely forgot his mother's request and returned home empty handed. Again and again his mother asked him to bring a relic for her shrine and on each trip he returned again empty handed. Over the months, his elderly mother become desperate to have some relic before she died, so one day she said to him, " If you forget my relic one more time, upon your return from India, I will kill myself right before your eyes!"

But on his next trip, the son was again filled with worry and pre-occupation over his business and forgot once more. As he was walking down the road to his mother's house, he suddenly remembered her words. Fearing she might actually carry out her plans, he was in a quandary over what to do. On the side of the road he saw the dried out carcass of a dog. He quickly removed a tooth from the dog's skull, and carefully wrapped it in a fine silk cloth. When he arrived home, he said, "Look mother, look what I've brought you, a tooth of the Buddha Shakyamuni himself!"

His mother believed him and was completely ecstatic. She immediately placed the tooth on her Buddhist shrine and for the rest of her days fervently prayed each day and made constant offerings. It is said that the tooth made miraculous gems appear and that when the woman died, extraordinary signs manifested in the sky. The dog tooth in itself carried no particular blessing, but the power of the woman's faith, believing it to be the Buddha's tooth, caused her to receive the blessing of the Buddha's enlightened mind.

Reiki surrounds us and can be opened within each of us, but it is our faith in the power of Reiki, which can open our mind to the power and experience of it.

59 How long does it take to become a practitioner of Reiki?

Generally speaking once a person has received the Reiki attunements from a qualified Reiki teacher, one's Reiki ability is *'switched on'*. Therefore one could say, following the instructions, which are usually given over a series of weeks or as a weekend intensive, one is a practitioner of Reiki. Other schools call this stage; a 'Channel of Reiki'.

However, to become a skilled practitioner or to call oneself this with some confidence, then one should establish a foundation through direct 'hands-on' experience. This comes through personal practice and integration. Our school, *The International Institute for Reiki Training*, recommends each new student complete a minimum of 30 hours of hands on healing at our student clinic, and at least 3 months practice and integration before considering learning the next level. This includes an assessment and practicum to determine the student's level of understanding and proficiency. These practice hours usually take most students anywhere between three and six months to complete. In addition to this, students are encouraged to give daily self-treatments as well as attending to daily meditations and energy enhancing exercises, which are given at this level. It is only through on-going practice and time that one's personal relationship to Reiki is fostered. Whether one learns fast or slow the energy has its own time and no matter how well intentioned we might be, we all need to do the work. If not, then the system can become an intellectual pursuit.

Knowledge is important, but this should be married with practical experience.

For some students who already have an established background in other healing systems or forms of remedial massage, then the integration time frame may vary. Each student is encouraged to put in the hours before professing to be a practitioner of the sacred science.

60 | Can Reiki wear out and can you over energise someone with Reiki?

Reiki is an outer manifestation of divine healing energy and by nature is unlimited. It is not like a water well, which will dry up with overuse. Reiki is timeless, unlimited and abundant. There is plenty of Reiki to go around for everyone. As one utilizes Reiki more and more, one's experience of becoming Reiki, manifests more and more. The more you take, the more you receive. When treating others, one cannot over energize another with Reiki. There is no such thing as too much energy.

Some systems of healing stipulate that one cannot over energize certain areas of the body such as the eyes, for example. A practitioner of Reiki on the other hand can energize the eyes for as long as is necessary and no ill effect will ensue. Some healing systems also suggest that one should not give healing to small children, or during pregnancy, however this is not the case with Reiki.

You cannot give either yourself or another, too much energy and this certainly will not have any detrimental effects. Provided one is using what is regarded as a sound traditional Reiki approach, the energy of Reiki will not overload a person's energy system. For those who have experienced 'Reiki Marathons' or group treatments, which are administered by numerous practitioners, one can attest to the enormous benefits gained. If any side effects could be given by receiving too much Reiki energy, the recipient may feel somewhat spacey. To remedy this, one should drink some water, or eat some food.

A good treatment hint is to remember that each person's body is like a container, which needs to be filled to restore balance. Giving a person what they need, means giving Reiki for as long as the person requires. This is usually felt, as the Reiki energy tapers off during the treatment. Once the container is full, the treatment is complete.

Reiki is a safe system of healing and because it naturally restores balance to the amount necessary for each individual, one cannot give someone too much energy.

If someone is experiencing a tremendous amount of clearing as a result of continued treatments, it comes to a question of choice: *"Do I want more or do I wish to integrate what I have received before proceeding with further treatments?"*

Some teachers of Reiki suggest a minimum time to treat a specific area and in some books this is also stated. Where some confusion arises is that these time frames are taken literally and one might assume that it is a golden rule. For example, it is suggested that one should treat each hand position for exactly 3 minutes however this is just a general guide. If your hands felt like staying for 10, 20, or even 30 minutes in one area, then this is fine. It is also worth noting that if one is receiving regular treatments that each progressive treatment tends to have a snowball effect. With each successive treatment, the momentum increases, as does the benefit for the person concerned.

61 | What are the Reiki hand positions?

When Reiki made its way from Usui to subsequent teachers, one of the central components of the system became the placement of hands on the body and its sequence. Depending on which style of Reiki one learns, the teacher will instruct the student in the placement of hands on the body. This also applies to positions for self-healing.

The emphasis on hand placement and position is particularly prominent in the Western '*Takata*' style of Reiki. Various western schools endlessly debate over who has the correct hand positions when in actual fact, the emphasis on a regimented and controlled sequence is far removed from the original Usui system.

Some teachers will even go to the point of making sure that the practitioner's hands are placed on the prescribed position to the centimetre, yet this is not terribly important as the Reiki energy flows to the areas of most concern.

In the Western style of Reiki, the emphasis is on treating the whole body. Here the practitioner places their hands on all the major areas of energy flow as well as the major organs of the physical body, leaving nothing to chance. This includes a sequence of 12 hand positions on the front of the body, and 12 hand positions for the back of the body. Here, the view is that each part of the body receives the same amount of Universal healing energy, thus bringing about a total balance and harmony for the body's energy system. This practice of 12 positions was developed with Hayashi and was later adopted and slightly altered by Mrs. Takata. Curiously, this method of treatment is considerably different from that of Usui's system of treatment.

In the Japanese system, (which reflects Usui's methodology) called

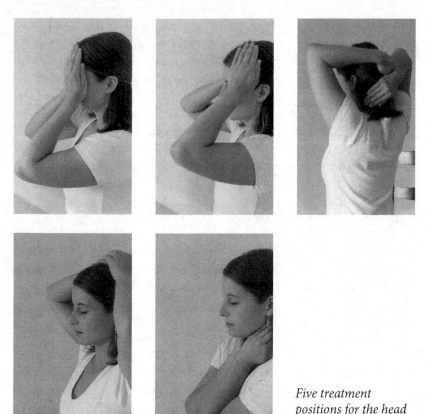

*Five treatment
positions for the head
and neck*

'*Usui Reiki Ryoho*' the emphasis is based on the practitioner's ability to perceive areas of imbalance. One school, the Japanese *Reiki Gakkai* or the Original Reiki society, teaches five specific hand positions for the head. These include (Jap.): *Zento-bu:* (Forehead position), *Sokuto-bu:* (Side of the head position), *Koutou-bu:* (Back of the head position), *Enzui-bu:* (Back of neck position), and *Toucho-bu:* (Top of head position). As the head and brain governs the body, and subsequently (the senses, nerves and nervus system) the head is usually treated first. The theory being, that if the body is relaxed, the energy will be received at an optimum level. Other than these basic hand positions the use of specific hand positions is not stressed in the Japanese style of Reiki.

Usui used a number of different methods for applying Reiki healing to the body. In Frank Arjava Petters book, *The Original Reiki Handbook*

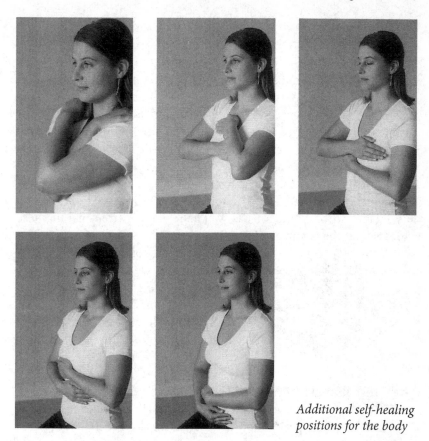

*Additional self-healing
positions for the body*

of Mikao Usui, Usui's *Hikkei* is presented and illustrates the various general treatment positions, which correspond to various ailments. This handbook is really a guide for practitioners wishing to learn where to place their hands that correspond to the various organs and areas of the body. For example, if one wanted to work on the large intestine, the placement of the hands would be situated in this area. For more experienced students, Usui taught specific methods for perceiving illness through methods of direct perception. Some of these methods exist today and are taught in the Japanese 'Reiki Ryoho' style, which reflects more closely the way Reiki is administered on an intuitive level.

Above are some photos of how one might facilitate a self-treatment utilizing a series of hand positions to cover all of the major areas of the body.

62 Do Reiki practitioners use a code of ethics and is there an international standard of practice?

Many Reiki schools adhere to a standard code of ethics and practice, which one often finds alongside any complementary therapy. These include: client confidentiality, ethical behaviour, and not to prescribe or diagnose unless licensed to do so. Other standard ethical codes include: maintaining the therapeutic relationship by not breeching the clients trust or safety, exhibiting humility, presenting a professional profile, as well as maintaining a high degree of personal cleanliness and hygiene. One refrains from the use of alcohol, drugs or other intoxicants during any therapeutic consultations as well as refraining from making false claims about the possible effects of Reiki.

Many Reiki schools have their own version of the Code of Ethics, although there is no one governing code which spans all schools. To give a general example, the following are the Codes of Ethics held by *The International Institute for Reiki Training*.

The International Institute for Reiki Training's Code of Ethics

1. IIRT practitioners shall conduct themselves in a professional and ethical manner, perform only those services for which they are qualified, and represent their education, certification, professional affiliations and other qualifications honestly. IIRT practitioners do not in anyway profess to practice medicine, psychotherapy or related practices, unless licensed to do so.

2. IIRT practitioners shall maintain clear and honest communication with their clients, and keep all client information, whether medical or personal, strictly confidential.

3. IIRT practitioners shall discuss any problem areas that may contravene the use of Reiki, and refer clients to appropriate medical or psychological professionals when indicated.

4. IIRT practitioners shall respect the client's physical/emotional state, and shall not abuse clients through actions, words or silence, nor take advantage of the therapeutic relationship. IIRT practitioners shall in no way participate in sexual activity with a client. They consider the clients comfort zone for touch and for the degree

of pressure, and honour the client's requests as much as possible within personal, professional and ethical limits. They acknowledge the inherent worth and individuality of each person and therefore do not unjustly discriminate against clients and fellow Reiki practitioners.

5. IIRT practitioners shall refrain from the abuse of alcohol and drugs. These substances should not be used at all during professional activities.

6. IIRT practitioners shall strive for professional excellence through regular assessment, personal development and by continued education and training.

7. Equality is practiced by all IIRT practitioners, regardless of which level of practice (including teachers/instructors), within the institute and related projects.

8. IIRT shall honour all other recognized and legitimate Reiki systems, practitioners and teachers regardless of personal differences and beliefs.

9. IIRT practitioners shall refrain from making false claims regarding potential benefits of Traditional Reiki.

10. IIRT practitioners shall in no way endeavour, either by personal act, word or deed, to bring the IIRT or its teachers and tradition into disrepute.

63 | What are the Reiki Principles and where did they come from?

Usui originally taught the Reiki Principles or Precepts of Reiki when Reiki began to gain wide-spread popularity in the early 20th century. Usui adopted these principles from *'the guidelines for a fulfilled life'*, written by the Meiji Emperor of Japan (1868-1912). For many practitioners in the West, these five Reiki principles have always been presented by Mrs Takata in the following way:

Just for today, do not worry. Just for today, do not anger.
Honour your parents, teachers and elders.
Earn your living honestly. Show gratitude to every living thing.

These Principles were later discovered at Usui's memorial in Japan and were found to be quite different in their writing. The following are those admonitions, taught as the Reiki Principles/Precepts/Ideals. It is interesting to see the variations from the various Reiki organizations, even in the translated version (from the original document in Usui Sensei's handwriting).

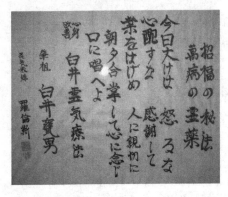

The Reiki Principles in Japanese Kanji

From Usui Sensei's memorial, 'when it comes to teaching, first let the student understand well the Meiji Emperors admonitory, then in the morning and in the evening let them chant and have in mind the five admonitions which are:

Do not get angry today.
Do not be grievous.
Express your thanks.
Be diligent in your business.
Be kind to others.

Here is another more literal translation, which includes the Japanese words with their translation:

Shou fuku no hiihou
Inviting blessings of the secret method

Manbyou no Rei yaku
Many illnesses of the spiritual (heavenly) medicine

Kyo dake wa Ikaruna
Today only anger not

Shinpai suna Kansha shite
Worry not with appreciation

Gyo wo hageme Hito ni shinsetsu ni
Do work to people, be kind

Asa yuu gassho shite kokoro ni neji Kuchi ni tonaeyo
In morning and night hands held in prayer, think in your
mind, chant with mouth

Shin shin kaizen, Usui Reiki Ryoho
Mind body change it for better Usui Reiki method

Chosso Usui Mikao
Founder Usui Mikao

If one attempts to place these admonitions into modern English, the
precepts translate as follows:

The secret method of inviting blessings
The spiritual medicine of many illnesses
For today only, do not anger, do not worry.
Be grateful. Endeavour your work. Be kind to all people.
In the morning and at night, with hands held in prayer,
think this in your mind, chant this with your mouth.
The Usui Reiki method to change your mind and body for the
better

The founder
Mikao Usui

Over the years, many Reiki schools have placed a great deal of
importance upon the Reiki Principles and many have built up all kinds
of teachings surrounding them.

Back in the days when most westerners considered the teachings
of Mrs. Takata to be the only link to the Reiki tradition, the Reiki
Principles was one of the few written Reiki teachings. Due to Mrs.
Takata's proclamation that Reiki be maintained as an oral system of
teaching, very little written material existed, and as a result, these few
precious lines for many became enshrined.

If one contemplates the precepts, one can find much inner meaning.
These universal ideals appear in all but a few religious systems and in
many regards, are quite useful, being based in common sense. It is no
wonder that Usui adopted them.

64 | Should I charge for Reiki and if so, how much?

A common question which arises in the minds of many practitioners and teachers is the issue of Reiki and money. *Should I charge for something, which is spiritual, a gift from the Universe?* The answer is that we cannot place a price on the Reiki energy itself, but it is important to place a price on our time and effort whilst facilitating a treatment. It is important that some form of exchange occur. For some, the exchange is in the form of money, for others it is in the form of material exchange and for others still it comes in the form of exchanging of services or a form of barter.

Often people feel uncomfortable about charging for Reiki and these issues usually stem from feelings of unworthiness, or the view of being the *'spiritual martyr'*. Other views come from the idea that anything spiritual should be free and attract no fees, as this will otherwise somehow taint the spiritual experience. However, these ideas hold no basis. Even in eastern societies there is always an exchange, whether this is in the form of a donation or via a benefactor. In order to give teachings and energy, money is the cog that turns the wheel.

It is also important that some form of exchange takes place so as to prevent a negative karmic debt being created by the recipient of services rendered.

If we as practitioners neglect to charge for our services, we in effect create a negative karmic debt for the very person we are trying to heal. They owe us for our time and energy. If we do not offer a space for exchange they create a karmic debt which will sow a negative karma in their future.

In the western world it is often hard to set fees based on a student's ability to pay. For what is months of careful saving for some is but a small fee to a wealthy person.

In a modern world we must contemplate the value we place on things. How many of us consider the money we pay for clothing or a new CD, and how many of us would quite easily purchase on a whim, a number of consumer items, yet when it comes to purchasing training or healing sessions for personal growth, our enthusiasm falls way short. I believe the greatest investment one can make in this life is the investment of our minds, for this is the only lasting thing. In the Dharma we are taught about the law of impermanence. All material items are subject to decay and change. Our precious human life is fleeting and we are all subject to old age, sickness, and finally death. If we set aside our desires and wants and allow ourselves to give out of generosity, how might we benefit from these actions? If not directly, we will at least sow the seeds of positive activity in the future.

65 | How often do I need to practice to maintain the Reiki energy?

Reiki is a system of healing where once you have the attunements, you have the ability to transfer healing energy for life. In effect, one cannot lose one's Reiki ability if it is not practiced daily. The attunements act like a door. Once the door is open the energy is flowing. Naturally a student can do much to increase the connection and this is best demonstrated through regular Reiki practice.

Although we will not lose any of our connection to Reiki by failing to do regular practice, we will miss out on the opportunity to develop ourselves by not practicing. It is a bit like building a fit body. If we simply think that we get fit by watching others or by wishful thinking, then we will make little progress. Fitness is achieved though regular attendance to a daily programme. If we think we will be fit if we simply do 5 hours running once a month, the benefit will not be as lasting as if we did twenty minutes, once per day. So regular practice, as they say, *makes perfect!* You become a perfect example of Reiki energy by active use of it in daily life.

66 | Is there any time where Reiki would not be safe?

Reiki is always safe. If one uses the practices of the system as they are given only benefit will ensue. Reiki does not require anything else from any other system of healing. Reiki is a non-dualistic system of healing and can only bring about a positive healing effect. Where Reiki could become unsafe is when the system has either been adjusted from its former roots or if other systems are combined into the practice.

When we mix or co-join the tenets of other systems, (which may be dualistic in nature), the practitioner cannot be certain of the outcomes. Some methods create openings in the energy system, whilst other systems summon outer influences, which may in turn create obstacles to healing. This is why it is essential to be sure you have the correct and authentic training in Reiki. Then one can rest assured of the beneficial effects, no matter what the situation might be.

67 What are Reiki Guides and do I need to know my guides to learn Reiki?

Many people have this idea about Reiki guides and that one needs to have a relationship to some outer guidance in order to be an effective healer. This concept of Reiki guides has sprung up out of the new age movement and has no origin in the Reiki system of Usui. Some people identify with outer forms and assign these outer forms with identities. In all but a few cases, we should consider guides as simply being archetypes of our own mind. This is not to discount those people who have identified with outer guides. It is important to simply be aware of our minds and our human tendency to give our personal power over to an outer idea.

If we feel like we are receiving direction from what is perceived as an outer influence or entity, one must first determine the quality of the information we are receiving. If we are certain that we have made contact with a higher power, one should test it. If you can determine with some accuracy, information which is beyond your knowing then you might have something useful to work with. If on the other hand, your Reiki guide knows what you know, then it is more likely that your intuition is manifesting on an outer level as a creation of your own mind.

If we take a more grounded approach then we will be more able to be a clear channel for Reiki. When one becomes involved in the spiritual realm, one can become confused and encumbered with many ideas and projections. We think that we are receiving all kinds of messages from somewhere else and begin to rely on the messages of others, rather than generating our own self-reliance and wisdom.

When we focus on our personal development and attend to our own healing, we can drop more and more of these ideas. This is a way to spiritual maturity, and with this our ability to heal others in meaningful ways will also increase.

7

Reiki experiences and the Chakras

68 Why do some people who receive Reiki experience various colours?

Seeing colours during a treatment indicates the mind of the individual perceives the subtle movements of energy on a visual level. Although not everyone sees colours, the interaction of the Reiki energy with the recipient's energy field can reveal its free play through the perception, in this case, through colours. The energy of Reiki can be measured as a particular frequency or field of energy. This band of energy has many more subtle and finer frequencies within it and these can be seen as various colours. When one perceives colour, it is these finer frequencies manifesting with the recipients energy field. Each colour is moving at a specific rate, the higher the frequency, the lighter the colour. For example, if you take a wheel of the spectrum and spin it, the movement of these colours merges into the colour white. Although there are many metaphysical correlations of what each colour means, one should simply recognize these visual manifestations as a bi-product of working with Reiki energy

69 What does it mean when someone's body twitches during a treatment?

Body twitches indicate a kinesthetic response to Reiki. This energy experience also indicates a de-armouring of the physical body. This is usually associated with the purification of unbalanced energy within the body. When these energies find balance, a sudden jolt or twitch can occur. During a treatment, the body begins to relax more and more, and these movements indicate tension leaving the body.

70   What does it mean when my eyes flutter during a Reiki treatment?

The fluttering of the eyelids is an indication of a change in the person's state of consciousness. Reiki directly affects our state of consciousness. As the energy affects our brain, it shifts into slower cycles. These brain waves or cycles have been described as Alpha waves. Once the Alpha state is reached, the signal of this state change is experienced by the eyelids fluttering. The eyes fluttering are termed: R.E.M. (rapid eye movement). This can be readily observed when treating others.

71   When I give Reiki, why do I feel the need to yawn?

The need to yawn during a Reiki treatment is a common experience. Yawning is another way that Reiki expresses itself as the flow of energy moves through the body.

Yawning is also representative of the vital energy moving into the energy body of the recipient. In Buddhist cosmology it is said that yawning is an indication that there is an opening of insight within the mind. It has also been shown that yawning represents that the body is relaxing. We all know how it is, we yawn when we are tired, we yawn when we are bored or when we simply want to ready ourselves for sleep. To yawn is to relax and this is in keeping with the element of deep relaxation that both the giver and recipient experience whilst facilitating Reiki.

72   What are the Chakras and how do these relate to Reiki?

The Chakras are subtle energy points within the human energy system. The word 'Chakra' is a Sanskrit word, which translates as: wheel, centre or eye and describes a nexus of energy, which governs the movement of energy flow throughout the body. If we think of Reiki as the electricity, then the Chakras are the transmitters.

Each Chakra vibrates at a specific frequency and each Chakra is affected by light, colour and sound. The Chakras can be affected by these means and other vibrational frequencies; and it is these frequencies, which affect the Chakras by means of sympathetic resonance.

The Chakra system also corresponds to the endocrine system of the body. The endocrine system controls the hormonal balance within human beings and it is these hormones which have a strong effect on our emotions.

Different spiritual traditions have many systems surrounding the Chakras. The more common view taught in the western style of Reiki borrows the classic system from the Hindu tradition. Here seven major points of energy flow are indicated, these being:

1. The Base Chakra
The Base Chakra is situated at the base of the body, at the perineum muscle. The Base Chakra governs the supply of energy to the reproductive organs, the kidneys, the adrenal glands and spinal column. The Base Chakra relates to our will to live, survival, procreation, family law, fight-flight response and our basic human instincts. The corresponding colour is red.

2. The Sacral Chakra (Hara Chakra)
This Chakra is situated three finger widths below the belly button and protrudes from the front, and back of the body. It is related to our emotions of sensuality and sexuality. This Chakra is related to our drive in the physical world and supplies our immune system and sexual organs with additional power. The Sacral Chakra is the seat of our personal power. The corresponding colour is orange.

3. The Solar plexus Chakra
The Solar Plexus Chakra is situated where the rib cage meets in the lower chest. Like the Sacral Chakra, it protrudes from the front and back of the body. This Chakra is related to issues of personal power, self-esteem/ self image and our emotional selves. It is linked to the gall bladder, the digestive system and the pancreas. The corresponding colour is yellow.

4. The Heart Chakra
The Heart Chakra is located in the centre of our chest. This centre governs our ability to give and receive love. Here is the seat of

compassion, giving, self-sacrifice, and unconditional love. The Heart Chakra governs the heart, the thymus gland, the circulatory system and lungs. The corresponding colour is green or pink.

5. The Throat Chakra

The Throat Chakra is located in the centre of the throat and protrudes from back and front of the neck. This centre governs communication and our ability to speak our truth and voice our opinion. The corresponding colour is deep blue.

6. The Brow Chakra

The Brow Chakra is located at the centre of our brow, between our eyebrows and the original hairline. This Chakra protrudes from the front and back of the head. This Chakra governs our intuition and intellect. It is the active centre of our imagination and our abilities of clairvoyance and psychic ability. This Chakra also relates to our pituitary and pineal glands. The corresponding colour is indigo.

7. The Crown Chakra

The Crown Chakra is located eight finger widths from the original hairline and is directly vertical to the tips of the ears when drawn directly upwards. The Crown Chakra governs our attributes of spiritual potential and universal understanding. Other related factors include: wisdom, clarity, oneness, unity and the interconnectedness with all life. It is our source of life and the activation point of the Reiki energy. The corresponding colour is, purple, gold or white.

If you have an interest in exploring the use of Reiki directly with this particular Chakra system, I recommend the book: *'Reiki and the Seven Chakras' by Richard Ellis. (Vermilion).* His explanation and knowledge of the Chakras is insightful, useful, and well worth the read.

73 | Is there only one system of the Chakras?

The Chakras are explored in many different ways and depending upon the system you encounter, opinions and theories will vary and in some cases contradict. To give you an example from Tibetan Buddhism, these centres are addressed in the following way: Here five major points are indicated and the associated colours or vibrations differ considerably to the Hindu model.

The first of the five is the centre called: 'Body'. This centre is situated in the middle of the head. As the brain governs the functioning of the body, this centre is given the name for this reason. This centre has 32 major energy channels, corresponding to the functioning of the brain. Its colour is clear and is accompanied with the syllable '*OM*'. If you hold your hands on your head and tone the sound *OM*, you should be able to feel your head vibrate with this sound. Certain sounds resonate with certain areas or centres of the body. Try it for yourself, it's an interesting experience.

The next area of this system is the centre of 'Speech'. This is located in the throat centre and has 16 energy channels, which govern the functioning of our speech. The colour associated with this area is ruby red and the corresponding sound is '*AH*'. Again hold your hands over your throat and tone the sound *AH* your throat should vibrate with this syllable.

The third centre is that of '*Mind*'. This is located at our Solar Plexus, in the lower, to middle portion of our chest. This centre has 8 major energy channels, two of which link to the eyes. Here the saying: '*the eyes are the gateway to the soul*', brings real meaning. This is why when we feel moved with heartfelt joy or sorrow for the matter, tears well up in the eyes. The corresponding colour is sapphire blue and the sound is the syllable '*HUNG*'. When one holds the hands in this place and makes the tone *HUNG*, one feels a vibration in this area.

The fourth centre is that of '*Qualities*'. This area is located at our belly button and has 64 major energy channels corresponding to artistic and creative qualities. If one has ever felt an affinity with a creative project, one will often feel a flutter in the belly. Here the colour is yellow and the sound syllable is '*SO*'.

Lastly, the fifth centre is located four-finger widths below the navel, in the centre of the body. This centre represents the centre of '*Activity*'. This is a power centre, which has either one or two major energy channels depending upon your sex. For women, there is one energy channel located at the G-spot. For men, there are two. One located at the prostate gland when unaroused, and the other at the tip of a man's 'noble tool' when aroused. Here the colour associated with this centre is green and the sound is '*HA*'.

Placing your hands on these areas and imagining the associated colours and toning the associated sounds is an excellent practice, which assists in balancing and harmonising the bodies' energy system.

Tone: **OM AH HUNG SO HA.**
Visualise: **Clear light, Red, Blue, Yellow and Green.**
Contemplate: **Body, Speech, Mind, Qualities and Activity.**
Meditating like this creates a unity and balance throughout the whole body and mind. These centres of energy and light are linked by the central channel, which is often imagined as a thin hollow tube of light blue. It is situated from the top of the head, running through the centre of the body, to the base, linking all five energy centres.

In total there are 72,000 minor energy points throughout the entire body and each point has a specific function for wellness and balance.

To illustrate an experience of our energy channels, which is common to many, we can use the example of an accident. If you have ever experienced a near accident, one can feel these energy channels moving. Here one experiences goose bumps, hair standing on end, and tingling throughout our arms and legs. As the fear of injury or death is recognised as not being real, these energies return to their normal place. Our bodies contain a complex energy system. In all the ways we interact with our outer environment, as well as our inner thoughts, feelings, and actions, have an intimate effect on this system. The direct application of Reiki to the energy centres has a noticeable and beneficial effect, no matter which view we hold.

74 How can I balance the Chakras with Reiki energy?

A simple way to balance the Chakras is by using the Second Degree Reiki symbols. Alternatively, one can simply place the hands over these areas and visualize the associated colours. The procedure is as follows:

1. Draw the Connection symbol over the Chakra.
2. Draw the Harmony symbol over the Chakra.
3. Draw the Power symbol over the Chakra.

• Place palm over palm, doubling the hand Chakras over each energy centre.
• Visualize each symbol (steps 1 to 3) and leave the hands at the Chakra point for approximately 5 to 10 minutes.*
(*Alternatively, visualize the associated colours for each centre, see previous 2 questions.)

To finish a session, ground your client by gently massaging both feet and allow them some time to come around.

During a Chakra Balancing treatment it may be that only a few points may require balancing, however as a sequence, this procedure aligns the individual and deeply touches the core of each centre and our being. Therefore we balance each centre from the Crown Chakra to the Base Chakra.

This is a very powerful technique for balancing the Chakras. It can be used instead of a full treatment or for one's self-healing. It can also be combined into your hands-on healing treatment or combined with absent healing procedures.

75 | Can I balance my own Chakras with Reiki?

The same procedure that we use on another can also be applied to ourselves. This process deepens our connection with our energy centers and establishes a deep calm throughout the process.

We begin in the following manner:

1. Draw the Connection symbol over your crown Chakra.
2. Draw the Harmony symbol over your crown Chakra.
3. Draw the Power symbol over your crown Chakra.

- Place palm over palm, doubling the hand Chakras over each energy centre.
- Visualize each symbol (steps 1 to 3) and leave the hands at the Chakra point for approximately 5 to 10 minutes.
- Now repeat the whole process for each Chakra centre. Brow; Throat; Heart; Solar Plexus; Sacral; and Base Chakra.

If you are a First Degree Reiki practitioner, then the symbols as mentioned previously, can be substituted with the corresponding colours:
Crown – Indigo
Brow – Purple
Throat – Blue
Heart – Green
Solar Plexus – Yellow

Sacral – Orange
Base – Red

76 | How long should I wait between Reiki levels?

Regarding the time taken between Reiki levels, this is largely the decision of the student, although in some cases a teacher may refuse a student if they have not completed sufficient practice or time between their previous levels. Many Reiki schools maintain that a student should spend time integrating and practicing a level until they have a sound understanding and experience before taking on new practices.

Many traditional Reiki teachers agree that this is sound advice. Some schools recommend an approximate three month period between First and Second Degree Reiki, and a year between Second and Third Degree. This recommended time frame offers time for practice. On the other hand, some students like to spend a year or two between First and Second Degree, whilst others like to spend as little time as possible so that they can learn each successive level in a speedy fashion.

One could consider it an obstacle to learning if not enough time is taken between Reiki levels. It is considered that one will potentially rob oneself of the spiritual development if the system is rushed. Much like grading a student in martial arts before the student is ready, the level of experience will not be fully matured and therefore the student will not pass the grading. Although many schools do not grade a student's ability, others do to ensure proper development.

8

The Reiki Attunements

77 | How do the Reiki attunements work?

Already in this book I have mentioned some ideas surrounding the attunements and how they are an essential part of conveying the Reiki ability to another. But to further elucidate, the process of attunement works like this. The teacher holds the key to aligning the student to Reiki. This transference is given in the form of the Reiki attunement. It is given by the teacher to the student and awakens the pathways of energy within the student's energy body. When this alignment is successfully conveyed, the student has this ability 'switched on' and can utilize this ability immediately for healing oneself and others.

Depending on who you talk to, the way of administering this alignment will vary tremendously. The most common form utilizes Reiki symbols, which in effect acts as a key to unlock the pathways of energy within the student's energy system, thus creating this alignment. Much like using the right key to unlock a door, the attunements enable the once closed door to healing energies to be open, and then the student can step through into the house of the healer.

Other forms of Reiki attunements utilize the placement of hands at certain places within the human energy field or 'Aura' to bestow the ability. In Japan the ceremony that opens the student to the energy flow is called 'Denju'. Within this ceremony the actual transmission of energy is called 'Reiju'. This method does not utilise the symbols, rather through regular Reiju the students Reiki ability is activated and with time and regular practice the students healing ability increases.

Whichever method of initiation or attunement is used, the person bestowing the attunement, their ability, method and level of personal accomplishment all have a bearing on the recipients Reiki ability.

Before you receive attunement to Reiki, carefully examine your teacher's methods and style, for they are responsible for awakening your healing ability. If a teacher does not have the right methods, little or no Reiki ability will result. This is why it is so important to know what you are receiving and from whom.

78 Can people receive a connection to Reiki without the Attunements?

For the most part the answer is 'No'. In order to establish a lasting connection, one does require a transmission from a qualified teacher. The Reiki attunements awaken the pathway to ones Reiki ability. And no, you will more than likely not gain the Reiki ability from reading this book. As the ability is passed via teachers who carry the Reiki lineage, the connection must come this way.

Now many people would argue that they have experienced healing effects without formally taking instruction and attunement from a teacher of Reiki. Here many people make the assumption that the healing energy they are utilizing is in fact Reiki energy. One could argue this point for a very long time however we might assume that if a person has not received initiation into the Reiki lineage, nor have they received the methods, the energy they are using could be better described as another form of healing energy.

It is possible (in some cases) that spontaneous openings may occur, however the results are usually not lasting or require the individual to maintain focus for the healing energies to flow. Having said this, some people do have a natural gift, yet even those that do, can certainly increase their ability and success by receiving the Reiki attunements from a qualified teacher.

79 How many attunements are given throughout the entire Reiki system?

The number of Reiki attunements will vary throughout the major Reiki traditions however there are generally an agreed number of levels and attunements, which go with this. When we look at the First Degree in the Takata and Hayashi Reiki styles, the First Degree states that there are four attunements. These attunements are usually given at four separate stages of a two day seminar. One is usually given in the morning, and one in the afternoon each day.

In some Japanese schools, only one attunement is given at the First Degree. If we look at the teachings of the Reiki Gakkai, the attunements take the form of Reiju, which are given to students monthly, sometimes for years. Some students may even receive dozens of Reiju before progressing to another level.

For the Second Degree, the Western branches of Reiki, give only one attunement at the Second Degree. This attunement is said to increase the students Reiki ability 100 fold as well as give the transmission for the three Reiki symbols which are given at this level.

In other eastern Reiki schools, three separate attunements are given at this level, one for each of the three Reiki symbols.

Traditionally in the final and Third Degree most teachers give one attunement to initiate a teacher. Some schools however, split the Third Degree into two stages, creating an A and B side or in other cases a Third and Fourth Degree. The A side or Third Degree, represents the beginning of the teachers path. Here one is introduced to the Third Degree symbol and Third Degree practices. The B side or Fourth Degree represents the final attunement and permission for the Sensei's understudy to be a teacher in their own right. This level of training usually is served as a formal apprenticeship.

To confuse matters still, other Reiki systems teach seven levels which accompany additional Reiki attunements and symbols. These are said to aid the practitioner in achieving higher levels of spiritual development.

Yet beyond this, there are many other Reiki styles, which are mostly invented or channelled styles. Here large departures often take place from traditional Reiki. Many teachers of these styles profess to have new and improved, and more powerful streams of Reiki. This will often include the introduction of new symbols, invented attunement procedures, as well as many other new elements. To give you an example, I recently saw an advertisement in an American New Age magazine offering 64 Reiki attunements! The bottom line is one will often benefit regardless of which style you choose just use your discriminating mind to find the right style for you.

80 | What does one experience during an attunement?

Just as one may experience a variety of sensations during a Reiki treatment, so it is the same with Reiki attunements. In general the recipient of an attunement may feel a great deal whilst others may sense little more than a deep sense of relaxation and warmth. Other participants describe feelings of joy; others are touched to the point of being speechless, whilst others become acutely aware of every sensation in their body and mind.

Each attunement brings with it a specific vibration and each persons energy field in union with this, generates a specific energy result. The important thing to remind ourselves is that no matter what experience we have, it plays little importance in our Reiki ability. The goal is not our sensational experiences. The goal is healing and benefiting others.

81 | What happens during the initiations and why do I have my eyes closed?

In some Reiki traditions it is a popular practice to let the students know that their eyes must be closed in order to receive the Reiki attunements. The truth of the matter is this is not a requirement for an effective transmission. Though having said this, closed eyes can be of benefit. The reasons are as follows. On behalf of the student, when the eyes are closed, ones attention and awareness is directed inward and with this, the student may be more readily able to sense what is arising in the mind as a result of the attunements. One misconception about eyes closed is that the student must not see what the teacher is doing, and that this will somehow disturb the attunement process, yet this is an erroneous view. If anything, a teacher of Reiki is more able to concentrate on what he or she is doing if they do not have a student *'eye-balling'* them, when they require their full concentration.

The other point to mention is that some teachers of Reiki consider it somewhat taboo to mention any aspect of the attunement procedure, and that it must remain a closed secret. When teaching others, I personally make a point of demonstrating one attunement before the class, describing the stages (not in full) but enough to quell curiosity before getting down to giving the Reiki attunements.

82 What if I don't feel anything during the attunements?

If you do not experience a great deal don't assume you are now cut off from your feelings, some attunements hold little outer sensation. Even if you do not experience one thing, something has occurred one need only examine the end result that the Reiki is working. There is little importance that should be placed on such experiences. When students share experiences, one of the common things is that ones mind gets into comparisons. One might say: *"I saw amazing colours"*, the other might say: *"I saw nothing"*. Whatever unfolds for you during an attunement is for you. Do not be concerned with your experiences, or lack of them for the matter. Experiences are transitory, they come and they go. Like clouds forming and dissolving in the sky, thoughts arise in the mind, play around in space, and dissolve back into space.

83 What is the difference between a Reiki attunement and a Reiki treatment in terms of energy transference?

A Reiki attunement and a Reiki treatment is a given amount of energy. One can think that an attunement is like a big pill that you take which enables you to give others medicine. Receiving a Reiki treatment, on the other hand, is like a smaller pill, it works well for the recipient, but it does not allow you to dispense your medicine to others. Reiki attunements are generally more powerful as a form of energy transference. It is a short burst of energy, where a large and concentrated amount of universal energy is bestowed upon the individual. Reiki treatments can also be tremendously powerful, however the time frame is over a longer period and as a result the energy experience differs.

In some Reiki traditions, the Reiki attunements are given over and over again. This is not because the students energy needs to be 'topped up', but for the accumulated beneficial effects of many attunements. The attunements are a powerful way to purify obstacles to our personal growth. The more we receive, the greater clarity is experienced. An attunement is a concentrated energy. When it is passed into and through the recipient, the effect is a cleansing and revitalizing experience.

84   Is there a way to give yourself a Reiki attunement?

Once a practitioner has received the Third Degree attunement and the ability to attune others into Reiki has been bestowed, the same applies to oneself. When we think about how wonderful it is to experience the Reiki attunements, why would we leave ourselves out of the picture? In the First Degree, Reiki students are taught how to give Reiki self-healing treatments. This is not only a beneficial and essential part of Reiki practice it is also the most enjoyable. When we have been initiated into the Third Degree, self-attunements are a wonderful extension.

As part of this practice, the Third Degree practitioner gives themselves the Reiki attunements, numerous times. It becomes part of a spiritual practice for purification and personal development. Self-attunements can be given to oneself in front of a mirror, or via the distant healing method. Alternatively, one can give a self-attunement to oneself as the facilitator and recipient at the same time. This process can be visualized, or combined with *Mudra* (hand gestures), or simply facilitated in the usual manner. Whichever way is utilised, the effects are the same.

Imagine re-experiencing all the power of your Reiki attunements, at whichever level you desired, over and over. The effects are quite powerful.

85   What role does ritual play in attunements?

The ritual which often accompanies Reiki attunements, acts as a focal point for energy. In a sense a very accomplished Reiki Master does not need to rely on outer ritual, however, it acts as a container or structure for the procedure. Much in the same way of using a ladder to climb to the roof of a house, once you have reached your destination, you have no use for the ladder, except if you need to come down. Therefore, ritual in Reiki is a tool, a vehicle, if you will, which takes you to a place of union with Universal energy. The Reiki attunements are a deeply symbolic process. When we have a structure and form to these attunements, a consistent format for giving the attunements is useful. This is the ritual. It acts as a direct way to focus ones intent and to assist the facilitator in the stages of transmission.

I also feel that a student expects some kind of ritual process. For example, one could give someone an effective Reiki transmission at a distance and then say, *"Ok, you've got Reiki, go out and start healing".* You would find that most people would have trouble believing it, even though it is that simple. This is another reason why the Reiki seminars are important in ones development as a practitioner. Here people from all walks of life come together. At the end of two days, they have a life long healing ability, always at hand. They can have a direct experience, which is unquestionable. When one has direct experience, there no longer remains an idea or intellectual concept of Reiki, it becomes solid and real. It becomes personal. Ritual is a part of our lives. The rituals we do without thinking, the way we wash our hair, or brush our teeth. We have a sequence of events, a structure we live by. So it is the same, with things of a spiritual nature.

86 | What does a Reiki teacher experience when giving the attunements?

Giving Reiki attunements, especially many attunements can be best summed up by feeling *'wired and tired'.* The tiredness is not due to a depletion of the teacher's energy field, it is representative of the concentrated mental focus, which is required throughout the attunement procedures as well as teaching others in general.

The feeling of being 'wired' is that one is filled with so much positive energy that one may feel somewhat overwhelmed. Other common experiences are a heightened sensitivity to sound, colour and light. After teaching a class, I am not usually in the mood for a big night out. I follow the advice that I give to my own students and also take some time to be still, relax and nurture myself. The mind simply isn't up to too much else.

The main reason for these experiences is that the body, mind and emotions have been attuned to Reiki many times. The Reiki ability comes through the Reiki teacher before transferring to the student, so in effect one receives and channels a lot of Universal energy in a concentrated period of time. This can also translate as forms of purification, particularly for new teachers as they become accustomed to holding the higher energies in the body for extended periods of time. As the teacher is the one who is harnessing the Reiki energy, the teacher becomes the vessel for the energy, which is then transferred to the recipient. Although all kinds of sensations can be experienced during the attunements it is not necessary to over identify, it is simply a bi-product of the interaction with Universal healing energy.

I believe most teachers of Reiki would agree that giving another human being a Reiki attunement is a tremendous honour and a humbling experience. To be able to give others this ability is truly a great thing. One acts as a marriage celebrant of sorts. Giving Reiki attunements is like wedding people with Universal Healing Energy. The act of giving Reiki attunements is like giving wedding vows. It is a vow uniting the student and Reiki for a life-time of healing and this is deeply touching.

87 | What are the differences between the First, Second and Third Degree attunements?

As an overview, the main difference between Reiki attunements of the First, Second and Third Degrees is the amount of Universal energy a practitioner can access. With each successive attunement the channel of the practitioner opens more and more. Having said this, each attunement has a specific function. The First Degree attunement is the first opening, be this with one or four individual attunements. Here the student achieves a lasting connection and ability to heal themselves and others and effectively becomes a channel for Reiki.

In the Second Degree, it is said this level is a way to further increase ones Reiki ability. Many practitioners report an increase of healing ability and connection. The Second Degree in the Western or Takata tradition gives the attunement for the three Reiki symbols, which are given at this stage. This is usually given as one attunement, yet in other styles, three individual attunements are given, one for each of the three Reiki symbols of the Second Degree.

In the Third Degree, the attunement is given to empower the person as a teacher of the system and one is then granted the title of 'Sensei' or 'Reiki Master'. Many teachers feel uncomfortable with the title 'Master' so many simply refers to themselves as teacher and nothing more. At the Third Degree the transmission is also given for the Third Degree symbol. This acts as the pathway to awaken another's Reiki ability. In other cases the Third Degree is split into two stages, or an additional Fourth Degree is taught which confers the ability to teach and attune others. Further to this, some teachers give an additional Fifth Degree, which confers the ability and permission to teach and attune one of their own students as a teacher.

This model of attunement is but one of many and one will find much variation in opinion and procedure. This can even occur from one teacher to the next of a similar style. Regardless of the view, we must honour other systems, which differ to that of our own. Each way is valid and all healing traditions, even the ones, which have evolved out of Reiki, come from the all-pervading mind stream of healing.

88 What role do the Chakras play in the attunement process?

The Chakras or energy centres of the body act in a similar way to transmitters of a radio. When another is attuned to the Reiki frequency, each energy centre receives an alignment and is raised to match the level of the Reiki energy being transferred. Each Chakra is also purified which assists the individual in healing and letting go of disturbing emotions and fixed views, which cloud our true nature.

The major Chakras of the human energy field branch from the central channel. This begins eight finger widths from the original hairline to the upper, central top part of our heads. It finishes four finger widths below the navel. It can be thought of as a thin hollow tube of light, no wider than the width of our little finger. When we are attuned, this central channel is the circuit for the energy to travel to all the Chakras as well as the 72,000 minor energy channels of the body. Thus, a full alignment to Reiki energy occurs. This is the pathway for Reiki to awaken within the individual. In particular, the Chakras in the palms, crown, heart, and navel are awakened and thus hold the new energetic pattern of Reiki.

89 How do the attunements affect the human energy field?

The Reiki attunements increase the size and vitality of the human energy field. Ones normal vibratory rate is dramatically enhanced and many people comment on the change they sense in someone who has received the attunements. What they are largely sensing is the persons newly attuned energy field, which (in contrast to its previous state) is dramatically different.

When we receive a Reiki treatment, it is a given amount of energy.

One could think of this as someone drawing water from a well and giving it to you. The attunement, on the other hand, gives you a bucket where you can draw from the healing waters whenever you desire. The more we work with Reiki energy, the greater our energy field becomes.

If one has ever had the opportunity to be in the presence of an awakened spiritual teacher, one will often feel a presence. This presence felt is their *'power-field'*. All the accumulated merit of their spiritual path becomes a field of energy. In some cases, just being near a being like this can be very healing. One immediately feels calm and peaceful, and joy naturally arises in the heart.

The good news is that you too can be like this. Through continued practice and spiritual development, you too will shine and be a light unto others. It takes work, but we all have an enlightened nature. All we need to do is actively work for the benefit of others, and purify the obscuration, which cloud our minds.

90 | What is the 21-day integration process?

The 21-day integration process comes from Mrs Takata's story of Usui. As the story goes Usui spent a total of 21 days in solitary retreat on Mt. Kurama. Here it is said that Usui laid before him 21 stones to represent the passing of each day of his retreat and that on the dawn of each day he would throw away a stone to signal the end of each nights vigil.

Whether Usui actually did this or not will probably remain unknown. However it is well documented that when we do something each day over a 21 day or three-week period we form a solid pattern. So it is recommended that a new student practice self-healing each day for 21 days to integrate the attunements as well as form good habits in the practice of Reiki.

As for integration in general, much of the effects of the Reiki attunements seem to occur within the Reiki seminar itself. One will also sense changes for the three days, which follow. Then as the days pass, the integration process becomes more and more subtle. One can say that one is always integrating Reiki. It is a 'life-times' process. The more you do, the more you learn, the more you learn, the more Reiki becomes a part of who you are.

91 If I have learnt Reiki elsewhere and receive an attunement with another teacher, will this cancel out my previous Reiki attunement?

Any subsequent attunements that you receive from another qualified teacher can only increase and augment the connection you already have. There is no way to lose or over-ride a Reiki attunement. Sometimes people feel that they should only ever continue with the same teacher, even in cases where they felt they did not receive the kind of connection they desired. On the other hand, if one feels a good connection with ones teacher, then proceeding with additional levels is beneficial as this promotes continuity with the style and teachings.

It is unfortunate when some people suggest that if you switch teachers it will cancel out the previous attunements. This only demonstrates their limited view.

If the attunement procedures differ from one teacher to the next, (and more often than not they do) then it is highly recommended to review previous levels with the new teacher, as well as receive their attunements. For example, at *The International Institute for Reiki Training*, if a student approaches our school to further their training, and they have already received First Degree from another teacher, we recommend they be re-attuned in our style before proceeding with further levels. This ensures continuity and a sound connection to our Reiki lineage and style.

92 How is Reiki energy different to other energy healing systems?

Reiki differs from other healing systems, in that the methods, which are used to activate healing energy, are awakened within a person through the process of attunement. These energy attunements activate the person's healing ability. Unlike many other systems of healing, the practitioner does not need to maintain any kind of mental focus for the healing energy to flow. The healing energy is simply activated by touch. The Reiki attunements also activate a full alignment with Universal energy. Within a few minutes of receiving a Reiki attunement, one has a noticeable healing ability. Where other healing systems require many years of practice to achieve the same level of proficiency, Reiki can be activated for the person, on behalf of the Reiki Teacher.

Reiki is also a Lineage based tradition meaning one requires a direct transmission and empowerments from a Reiki Sensei or Teacher of the Reiki tradition.

Although the methods of Reiki have a precise practice and application, the healing forces utilized span many forms of healing. Be this in the form of the healing practices of a Shaman or hands-on healing in the Spiritualist Church, we must recognise that all healing energy ultimately comes from the one source. The difference being, the method to bring one in union with this healing ability and the mythologies utilised.

93   How does Reiki energy blend with other energy healing systems?

No matter which system of healing you learn; whether this was before or after learning Reiki, the Reiki energy will still come through your hands. Be this whilst giving a Massage, facilitating a Pranic Healing session or doing Tai Chi, the Universal energy can't help but flow once the attunements are in place. Reiki energy is with you for life and therefore becomes a part of everything you do. For example, if you are facilitating a Pranic Healing session and utilizing the methods taught, then Pranic energy will come through your hands and be transferred to your client. Yet at the same time, Reiki energy will also be flowing in parallel. If one has the intention to use Prana energy verses Reiki, then the awareness will be on the Pranic energy flowing. Although the Reiki energy is also flowing, one may not necessarily recognise it. Whichever healing style you practice remember that Reiki encompasses all things.

94   If I receive the Reiki attunements whilst pregnant, will my child be born with Reiki?

This is an interesting question. In my experience, the infant will receive a blessing and in some cases, the healing ability. Although no formal attunement is given in this case, mother and baby are united so it is possible for there to be a dual attunement. However, this does not necessarily mean that one will have an instant healer for a child. In any case, when the child is ready, they may receive formal training and Reiki attunements. Children can actually be attuned to Reiki at any age.

It simply becomes a matter of whether or not they have the attention span to participate. As a general guide, most children under the age of 10 years should be taught outside a formal class environment. If a child exhibits a tendency towards healing, then it is ideal for a parent or parents to learn. This way they can be an example for their child and their natural curiosity will in most cases follow. If the child is too young to sit still for the Reiki attunements, then distant attunements can be given as an alternative and the parent can then instruct the child in the rudiments of self-healing as well as helping others in informal ways.

Learning Reiki for children is a wonderful 'head-start' in life. It promotes self-reliance and confidence as well as a loving and caring attitude. I hope in the years to come that Reiki will be taught alongside science, maths, and the arts at a primary school level. The sooner one learns to be able to heal oneself, the better off we all will be.

9

Giving Reiki to others
Part 1

95 Can I pick up another's symptoms whilst giving Reiki?

Whilst administering a Reiki treatment, many different kinds of experiences can arise. One of these experiences is the feeling that one is sensing the symptoms of their client. This kind of transference does happen and can be experienced in a variety of different ways. On a physical level, one may feel depleted or a heavy feeling after the treatment. One may also feel a slight pain streaming up ones forearms. At other times, a practitioner may feel the symptoms of the patient, corresponding in their own body. For example, we may have our hands on a client who is suffering from a headache and begin to feel a pressure in our head. This is not to say that feeling a client's symptom is an active form of diagnosis which should be cultivated. Ideally, we can learn to perceive areas of imbalance without the necessity of experiencing these sensations in our own body. Sometimes when this kind of transference does occur, it is usually due to a breach in ones personal boundaries. This can be avoided by spending the necessary amount of time before a treatment establishing ones connection to the Reiki energy and thus ones boundaries are secure. Other common experiences of sensing clients' symptoms come in the form of visual imagery, internal dialogue, and emotional states.

96 | How can I identify this kind of transference?

If for some reason you experience transference from your client (but are unsure how to recognise this), the following are some steps to identify the problem.

1. Naming
If we find ourselves experiencing something which appears as being foreign, the first thing to do is to give expression to the sensation. If we feel a dull or heavy feeling in an area of our body, for example, the solar plexus, we can state: *"Here is dullness in my solar plexus"*. Often times by simply naming the sensation, this allows it to clear and we can simply carry on with the session.

2. Identification
Another approach is to ask the question when experiencing the sensation. *"Is this (name the sensation and its location) mine?"* After you have asked the question, just be still and relax, and allow the first impression that comes to your awareness. This might come in the form of a simple, 'yes' or 'no' answer, or another intuited response. Your intuition may give you feedback in terms of a feeling, colour or other sensation. If you receive a 'yes', then, simply thank your perception for this signal and state in your mind, *"I will deal with this at a later time"* then carry on with your session. If you receive an intuitive 'no' answer, then this is transference from your client. At this stage we can proceed with a similar approach. If the sensation is located in a particular part of your body, place your hands on the patient in the corresponding area. Now acknowledge this sensation as mentioned before and state: *"I thank my perception for signalling this symptom in my client, I now ask this symptom to leave my body"*. Often times this is sufficient for the signal to dissolve. On the other hand, if the symptom still resides, the following two steps will in most cases remove the transference.

3. Transforming
In the event that you have identified the transference from your patient, yet the previous methods have not cleared it, then proceed with the following: Take your hands off your patient and place them in the Gassho* position. (*hands held in prayer position at your heart centre.) Imagine that a clear and radiant sphere manifests in your

mouth. Imagine this sphere is a purifying energy. With a short sharp breath, blow this sphere between your hands. As it makes contact with your hands, it instantly dispels any lower vibration. Now bring your awareness to the place where you are experiencing the transference. Place your hands over this area, in Gassho position, but this time with your hands slightly apart. Imagine that between your palms manifests an identical clear, radiant sphere. As this is placed at the location of the transferred energy, imagine this sphere is magnetic and is attracted to the patient's transference in your body. See this sensation, emotion or illness drawing into the sphere, completely leaving your body in the form of black smoke. Once it makes contact with the sphere it is transformed and purified.

Continue this for as long as is required or until you feel clear. Now reconnect with the Reiki energy and imagine this coming into and through your body and continue your treatment. Connecting with the Reiki energy re-establishes your personal boundaries.

4. Averting

An alternative way to purify a client's transference is by averting the lower energy. Imagine this energy in your body in the form of a dark energy or simply focus on the sensation which brought it to your attention in the first place. Now in the centre of the lesser energy imagine a sphere of clear light manifests. Now as you '*breathe in*', the sphere becomes active and as you '*breathe out*', imagine you are breathing into the sphere, much like blowing up a balloon. With each out breathe the sphere increases more and more, until it encompasses the lower energy. As soon as the sphere makes contact with lower energy it is immediately transformed into light.

97 Is there a way of purifying the client's lower energies when normal Reiki healing is not sufficient?

It is not common that Reiki will not clear a lower energy. In most cases, it is simply a matter of spending the necessary amount of time in the area. However, if one wishes to use a more direct approach, the following technique will bring speedy results. If you are working on an area which seems to contain a very dense or heavy frequency, begin by placing your awareness on your solar plexus. Visualise a radiant sphere of purifying light in this place. Now imagine that clouds of positive Reiki energy gather above the top of your head. Each time you inhale, imagine this healing energy enters the top of your head and descends down through your central channel. When you exhale, imagine a healing energy is expanding this field of energy and light in your solar plexus. Now place your hands on or slightly above the area of imbalance on your client. Allow this sphere of energy and light to descend up through your central channel until it comes into your mouth. Now with one short, sharp breath, blow this sphere of healing energy into the area of concern. Place your hands on this area and now visualise that this powerful healing sphere is inside the very core of the imbalance. It instantly transforms this lower energy, dissolving it completely. This light also expands out to fill the entire body with this field of healing energy and light.

One can also extend this technique beyond the physical body to move this energy into the client's aura or as a way to touch and heal others near by.

98 | What are some ways to cleanse myself after a Reiki treatment?

It is only necessary to energetically cleanse yourself after a Reiki treatment if you feel you have something which needs to be cleared. Mostly after giving Reiki to another, both yourself and the recipient are feeling calm and peaceful. However, in the rare event that you do take on more than your share of lower energies, then it is advisable to do the following exercise.

Netting the lower energies
This practice is an effective way to clear lower energies. Imagine that you are sitting or standing upon a disc of clear light. This disc has a fine screen running through it like a tightly woven net. Now as you inhale the clear disc rises upwards through and around your body. As it moves upwards more and more (with each inhalation), imagine the disc is catching any lower energies in your body which are foreign. With each inhalation the disc rises more and begins to accumulate all lower energies as it goes. Finally the disc has risen above your head and your body is free from all disruptive energies. You now imagine all of these

lower energies in the form of various undesirable symbols sitting upon the clear disc above your head.

In the next stage you imagine that there is a blue sphere in your solar plexus. With one inhalation the blue sphere ascends your central channel through the centre of your body and instantly makes contact with these lower energies. Once contact is made the lower energies immediately transform into light which filters through the fine net and showers over and through your body, filling it with blue light. One may repeat this process as often as one likes or until one feels completely clear and energised.

99 | What use has salt in cleaning lower energies?

Salt is an effective natural transformer of lower energy which is why many people feel invigorated after a swim in the ocean. The use of salt as a means of purification has been used for centuries throughout many cultures. Simply immersing yourself in salt water cleanses much unwanted lower energies. In terms of healing work, one simple thing to do between Reiki treatments is to wash your hands with salt and water. First wet your hands and forearms, then rub salt*, (much in the same way you would wash your self with soap) then wash this off with fresh water. The emphasis is always on the downward strokes away from your body and one may also integrate awareness on the out breath as you discharge these lower or unwanted energies.

Another useful way to cleanse your energy field is to run a bath to a comfortable temperature and depth and add two generous handfuls of sea salt. Soak in the bath for 15 minutes. Now let the water out of the tub, and imagine with your 'out breath' that all the lower energies are leaving your body in the form of black sludge. All these unwanted energies are leaving your body as the water drains from the bath. Once the water has drained, finish with a shower. You may feel a little tired after doing this, so it is best to give yourself a Reiki self-treatment for 15 minutes to one hour afterwards.

---

* Be sure not to do this if you have any open cuts on your hands.

100 Can Reiki accelerate the bodies healing rate and if so, how does this work?

When we give ourselves Reiki or receive it from another, our body is charged with vital healing energy. When we have more vital energy available to us, we do not require as much of our own life force to maintain the functioning of a healthy body. An additional supply, if you will, is being administered through the treatment. One could liken it to drawing water from a well which is constantly being filled by an underground water steam, it therefore never runs dry and the water is fresh, clear and always on tap. When we have this supply of vital energy, this boosts the body's ability to heal at a faster rate. With the transference of Reiki energy, a natural balance is restored which leads to a healthy and functioning body.

Reiki also increases our vibratory rate to match the same frequency of the Reiki energy, which is the vibration of health and balance. The more we establish this connection through regular practice, the more this vibratory rate matches. The direct result is health and vitality.

101 What does it mean, when someone does not heal?

The issue of whether one is healed or not is often based on the expectation of the healer or recipient of the healing. Reiki can assist on many levels (not just the physical). The overall effect of a treatment can have long term effects, where the noticeable results filter out gradually.

For example a person may come with a specific injury and the symptoms do not seem to lessen, however, the client has noticed when asked about their general sense of well-being that they are feeling less stressed or are sleeping better. Another case might be that someone who comes for a treatment and a few days later, still have a cold, but they receive a job offer with better pay. In other cases, it simply might be that one treatment is not enough to make a noticeable difference. It is not uncommon that after a third or fourth treatment that some kind of breakthrough occurs.

102 What if the person has the wish to be well, and has received several treatments, but no matter how many, still the illness remains?

In the case where numerous treatments have not been successful, this often indicates a karmic cause to the healing process. Here one may simply require an alternative road to healing. In some cases, it makes little or no difference what one does the illness is part of that person's path or journey.

When this seems to be the case, one should explore other avenues. Although Reiki is a wonderful tool for healing, it is but one of many methods. Perhaps the client would be better suited to a Chinese Acupuncturist, or Naturopath, or General Practitioner. Just as it is wrong to dismiss other alternative methods, it is downright dangerous to think that western medicine should be utterly disregarded. The right view is to take the best of both worlds and to take the necessary steps where indicated.

103 Are there any contra-indications to the use of Reiki?

Over the years, Reiki has accumulated a number of myths concerning the contra-indications of its application to numerous situations. In truth, this is mostly *here-say* with little evidence to back such claims. Our physical minds tend to put limitations on how and where Reiki can be used. To illustrate an example, an established Reiki myth is that Reiki should not be applied to broken bones. The belief is that its power will immediately set the bone within minutes and if in a dislodged position will require re-breaking to set correctly. Reiki is fast working for pain however it is not like fast setting glue. If you have ever experienced what it is like to break a bone, you would offer a tremendous disservice by not offering Reiki. Reiki is always safe and it will not harm. One should use it freely with a clear conscience.

104 Can a practitioner transfer their own negativity to the client during a treatment?

When one is giving Reiki to another, the practitioner is simply a conduit for the healing energy. When one is aligned to the Reiki energy via the attunements, the energy manifests a protective field. In most cases our own energies do not interfere with this process and are rather raised to a higher vibratory level. One can actually be feeling tired or even mildly ill before administering a Reiki treatment, yet by the end, one will feel revitalised and balanced. Reiki heals the giver and the receiver. The energy must pass through the Reiki channel in order to transfer to the recipient, therefore both receive a treatment. Having said this, it is important to acknowledge when one requires self-healing. For example, if the practitioner was going through some difficult emotional issue and did not feel stable enough to give Reiki to another then it is important to listen to one's instincts and seek the care and guidance of a trusted healer or counsellor.

105 Are there some ways to create personal boundaries in healing work?

Before we give Reiki to another it is worth while considering our personal boundaries. Making some form of conscious connection with the Reiki energy is an excellent way to establish this connection as well as to psychically prepare oneself.

One way to do this is to imagine that there is a large sphere of energy above our heads. This sphere represents the unlimited power and healing energy of Reiki. We then imagine this light descends upon us, filling our very being from the soles of our feet to the top of our heads. Much like filling a vessel with water, our bodies become filled with Reiki energy. We next imagine this healing energy overflows out of our head and fills our entire energy field.

One can also enhance this experience by making strong wishes for a continued connection throughout the session and that what ever healing energies are beneficial may be for the highest good of all concerned.

Once we feel this connection and have prepared ourselves both mentally and energetically we are ready to begin the session. Working in this way establishes a sound personal boundary throughout the treatment.

106 Is it necessary to remove jewellery before a treatment, and can jewellery interfere with the flow of healing energy?

Reiki energy goes through anything and will not limit the energy flow. Keeping this in mind, for more practical reasons, if a practitioner has many bangles or a ticking watch, then the rattling of these items or ticking, particularly around the head positions can be a distraction for the recipient. For example, if the practitioner was placing their hands on or near the client's ears and was wearing a ticking watch or had several wrist bangles, the "tick, tick" or "clang, crash, bang!" of jewellery can do much to disrupt the otherwise peaceful atmosphere. Therefore, it is a good idea to be mindful of this and to remove all forms of jewellery before the treatment.

For the recipient, it is not necessary to remove their jewellery as this will in no way affect the healing energy being transferred. If anything, the objects will be empowered and blessed by the Reiki energy.

107 What are some guidelines for practitioners when treating others?

In terms of our overall physical presentation, it is a good idea that you be well groomed, and for the sake of general hygiene, wash your hands prior to and between Reiki treatments. Your finger nails should be clean and hair neat and tidy. For the sake of your client's comfort, it is also recommended that you avoid eating foods which are high on the odour list, such as onions and garlic. Ideally you should keep some breath mints handy and attend to using your underarm deodorant. Some hand positions also require a close proximity to the body and with this in mind it is advisable to be mindful of your client's sensitive noses. You should also not draw unnecessary attention to yourself, nor be outlandish in your appearance. Instead, display a humble disposition as this is in keep with the teachings.

108 How do I know when to move my hands to another position during a treatment?

The more we work with the Reiki energy, the more we begin to gain a relationship to it. When we are administering Reiki in a particular position, often it will feel like the area is drawing Reiki energy, much in the same way a dry sponge soaks in water. Once this area is full there is a sense that this drawing feeling subsides. This is an indicator that the area has received all that it requires. However one's sensation is not limited to this as many other indicators can arise for each individual. In most cases these indicators can even vary from person to person or treatment to treatment.

With ongoing practice your hands will tell you when it is time to move to another position, but for the beginner a set amount of time for each position is a 'fool proof' way to give your prospective client, all the energy their body needs.

When treating others, sometimes a few minutes are not enough. If we are working on a specific injury for example, we may feel like our hands need to be in that one position for 20, 30, or even 45 minutes. When we are working on a serious illness, like a cancer or tumour, then we may feel as though these areas are drawing enormous amounts of healing energy. In such cases the experience many be considerable heightened and the length of time increased. The body will draw what it requires and it is the intelligence of the Reiki energy which determines the amount of and the vibration of energy to be transferred.

Gaining a greater sensitivity of what is required comes with practice and it is a matter of trusting what you sense during the treatment. Remember, you can not give someone too much Reiki, so it is better to give a longer session than not enough.

109 Why is it that both the practitioner and the client can become thirsty during and proceeding a Reiki treatment?

When the body relaxes during a treatment, it is not uncommon for this experience to arise. This is due to the assimilation of Reiki energy throughout the body. If you like, the Reiki energy is like electricity and in order for it to be easily conducted, a fully hydrated body is most beneficial. Water also assists with the cleansing of toxins from the body. When both the practitioner and recipient relax, the body begins its cleaning processes similar to the ones experienced when someone is sleeping. The body is simply telling you, that it requires water to assimilate this cleansing process.

Another point to consider is the amount of water one should drink. For treatments, I usually recommend that it is best to drink until you feel your thirst is quenched. A rough guide is two to three glasses before and after the session. This is recommended for both the practitioner and the recipient. Ideally eight glasses of filtered water per day which is free from chemicals is highly beneficial. Other varieties of water such as certified distilled water, fresh rain water or reverse osmosis are also ideal.

10

Giving Reiki to others
Part 2

110 Why do I sometimes feel comfortable receiving Reiki from one practitioner whilst not as comfortable with another?

When we encounter a new person we generally have three different kinds of response. These being: an attraction, an aversion, or a neutral feeling. Although most would identify strongly with outer appearances, such as the person's appearance, smell and so forth, we subconsciously respond largely with the individual's vibratory level. If we feel a strong attraction and instantly like a person, it is due to the fact that our vibratory matrix or energy field is compatible with theirs. This is called sympathetic resonance.

Equally, if we feel an aversion to another, this indicates that ones energy field is not compatible with the other. Much in the same way as magnets attract or repel, so too, it is the same with people. One can readily notice this when we meet someone we feel strongly attracted to. Likewise when meeting someone who instantly creates an uneasy feeling, we often cannot place the reason why, we just don't feel comfortable. Like attracts like, it is a Universal Law.

111 What can I do if I feel an aversion to another and what are some ways to look at this?

If you are presented with a situation where you feel an aversion to another, there are essentially three ways to deal with this. The first is to avoid the situation. If you do not feel as though your energies are compatible, remove yourself from that person's presence.

The second way to look at this is to generate the mind of compassion. We can think that this person is operating out of their own conditioning and so we take our perspective to a higher viewpoint. Here we develop compassion and see them as an opportunity for patience.

The third and highest view is to see them as a mirror. If they press our buttons, they hold a mirror to us. We see them as a teacher and examine our own minds. We may think: *"What great compassion they posses in showing me the areas I need to heal"*. If we can see them as having an enlightened nature, we see the potential in every situation and use this as the raw material for our own personal growth.

112 How can I increase sensitivity in my hands for healing myself and others?

The more you practice Reiki, the more sensitivity opens. However practicing some of Usui's Reiki techniques such as *'breathing though the hands'*, can assist in increasing this sensitivity.

The Japanese name for this practice is *'Gassho Kokyu-ho'*. It is a traditional method of breathing through the hands which increases sensory experience. A literal translation of Gassho Kokyu-ho is *'hand breathing'*. Gassho means, *'pressing one's hands together in prayer'*; Kokyu means, *'breath, respiration'*; and ho means, *'technique, method or way'*.

The technique is as follows:

1. Sit or stand in a comfortable position. Place your hands in Gassho position, calm the mind and say silently: *"I will begin Gassho Kokyu-ho now"*. Close your eyes and breathe calmly.
2. Now reach your hands, high above your head and connect to the fullness of the Reiki energy. (You can image your body filling with energy). One imagines that one is touching a vast field of energy and light. You can also imagine this is like an enormous planet, representing the unlimited power of Reiki. Once you have made this connection, slowly move your hands back to Gassho position.
3. Feel your breath flowing naturally and slowly drop your awareness to your Hara* and relax.
4. With your hands in Gassho, now imagine that in the space in front

of you a sphere of energy and light forms. This is roughly the size of a beach ball. Imagine this sphere in the colour blue and that the tips of your fingers are just inside this bubble of healing energy.

5. Begin to image that you are breathing through your hands. Whilst breathing in, imagine Reiki energy is entering your hands from the sphere in front of you. This blue light is streaming down through your fingertips and hands and streams up both arms. This energy meets in your upper chest and flows down your central channel, to your Hara* (Sacral Chakra). See this light expanding until the Hara is filled with energy.

6. On the out breath, imagine this light is moving from the Hara back along the same pathway to the hands and filling them with energy. This energy is then releasing in a burst of energy in all directions. With practice, you may feel a strong presence in your palms, tingling or pulsing. This breathing technique can gradually be drawn out to extended breathing cycles.

7. Repeat for 5 or 10 minutes or for as long as you like.

8. Once you feel this is complete, imagine that the blue field of energy and light condenses in space and merges completely with your hands and fills them with healing energy.

9. If you feel the need, shake your hands by the side of your body, up and down and back and forth. (This releases any unused energy or congestion as a result of this practice).

113 Is there a way to sense imbalances in the energy field?

The ability to sense imbalances is something that everyone can learn and with practice can be a useful tool in determining the direct application of hands-on healing. The following method is a way to sense these energy imbalances which manifest in the human energy field. This is another original method from Usui.

Byosen Reikan-ho is the Japanese name given to this method for sensing imbalances with your hands. The words Byosen Reikan describe the energy of a disease. It can be detected with your hands and will vary depending on the severity and condition of the disease. *Byosen*

---

* The Hara is the name given to a place of stored power. This is situated 3 finger widths below the navel.

Reikan literally means energy sensation of sickness (imbalance/disease). *Byo* means '*disease, sickness*' and Sen means; 'before, ahead, previous, future, precedence', Rei means '*energy, soul, spirit*' and Kan means; '*emotion, feeling, sensation*'.

When detecting a Byosen one will usually feel sensations such as tingling, tickling, pulsating, heat, cold and so forth; these sensations are called in Japanese: '*Hibiki*'.

Byosen Reikan-ho is a method of scanning for imbalances, which also goes one step further by actually removing the imbalanced energy which is a primary cause of the disease. Whenever disease is present there will be a Byosen, even in cases where the recipient is unaware of a physical condition. When sensing a Byosen in someone's body, one can then apply Reiki healing so that the related disease (or potential disease) will either completely heal or never manifest on the physical level. In cases where a disease is prevalent, this method with prolonged use will in most cases decrease the physical symptoms.

The technique is as follows:

1. Sit or stand comfortably next to the recipient.
2. Place your hands in Gassho, calm the mind and say silently "*I begin Byosen Reikan-ho now*".
3. Place your hands on or slightly above the body, move them around and take notice. What you are looking for are areas where you feel something different from the overall general sensation (i.e. heat, cold, tingling, an absence of sensation, etc.).
4. When you sense a '*Hibiki*', hold your hands over that area. The Hibiki will increase and then decrease; this is one cycle, which will repeat as long as your hands are on the body. The longer you hold your hands over a spot the more cycles you will feel; with each cycle, the peak of the Hibiki diminishes slightly. Keep your hands over the Hibiki for a minimum of one cycle.
5. Move your hands to the next Byosen and repeat step 4.

114 When giving Reiki, why can one side feel stronger than the other?

Reiki energy flows equally from each hand regardless of whether you are left or right handed. If one side feels stronger than the other it simply means that your awareness is greater on one side of your body than the other. In metaphysical terms we all have a male and female side to our bodies. Commonly known as 'Yin' and 'Yang', our left side represents our inward or receptive side, or female, wisdom aspect, and our right side represents our Yang or male, activity aspect. In other cases where we may have our hands in different positions on the body, an indication of greater energy flow in one hand may also correspond to an illness or injury. Whether it is a question of perception or an imbalance, one will find that the energy will balance on an equal level with practice and integration.

115 What is some advice for treating people with serious illnesses?

In the case where we are working on the seriously ill, then it is recommended that we find out as much as we can about the persons condition, and the easiest way to do this is by talking with the person prior to treatment. They can tell you more about their symptoms than anyone else it is their illness after all. Once you have determined the areas most in need, one may even consult with the person's physician. This is not always possible, but listening respectfully to their physician can reveal many things and it is important to honour this process by maintaining a humble disposition.

If treating a patient in a hospital setting, then in general it is best to place the hands in the area of most need and to do this without disturbing the attending staff, nor getting in their way. Often the situation arises where the patient will require a check up during the treatment, so where possible it is best to determine an appropriate time to give the person Reiki.

One should never establish false hope in a patient who is terminal. It is not our choice whether Reiki will heal them, or not. It may be that it is the person's time and the Reiki energy will allow them to pass in a peaceful manner. It other cases, it will steadily pave the road to recovery. We don't proclaim that Reiki will cure them, yet we also do not rule out this scenario in any case. A Reiki practitioner should in no way prescribe nor diagnose the patient. Nor should they interpret their experiences or criticize the patient in any way. Under no circumstances should the problems of family or work be introduced when a patient is recovering as this only brings worry and this certainly does not contribute to a speedy recovery. What does assist in recovery is a positive outlook. Have the patient talk of pleasant things, encourage them to engage in games, stories or watch films which are inspirational and positive. The more we feed our minds positive impressions the quicker we will heal.

If you are working on someone who is recovering from recent surgery, it is vitally important that you determine the appropriate level of touch. In some cases this may mean that you do not touch them at all, rather hold your hands just off the body and over the area of concern. If you are unsure or if the patient is not conscious, one should be mindful and lightly rest the hands and if in doubt, hold the hands above the area of concern and administer the healing energies this way.

When we are working with others who are seriously ill we also need to be aware of the immediate energetic surroundings of the patient and attend to our own energy needs. Hospitals and the sick room are often places where lower energies thrive. If you intend to open yourself up to healing another in an energetically polluted environment like this, then special attention must be adhered to when establishing your energetic boundaries. One should spend additional time centring and establishing a positive healing field. This will assist in the transformation and purification of these lower energies, should you encounter this situation.

In extreme cases, working on some patients can leave you emotionally and energetically drained, so it is also important to know when it is time to rest and when it is time to work. It is also not advisable to treat someone who is sick if you are suffering from a cold or flu. Besides the fact that you are the one who is probably in need of receiving Reiki and taking rest, you may endanger the patient by passing on your ill-health, thereby adding to their already weakened condition. This is the last thing a patient needs, so use your common sense.

It is also good advice to remember to say no if you feel you are already over committed with other patients. You do not have to save the world; work diligently and attend to your own needs. You are of little use to others if you fall sick due to burning your candle at both ends. A healer must take this into consideration if they are to sustain a good level of personal well-being on a daily bases.

116 Will my mundane thoughts interfere with the flow of Reiki energy?

At a very basic level, Reiki is activated by touch, so for Reiki healing to occur, one simply places their *'hands-on'*. The connection to the Reiki frequency also operates independently of your thoughts and emotions, so the quality of healing energy coming through the channel is not affected in any way by what is going on in your head. Having said this, it is better to focus your mind on healing. In our training programmes we give specific techniques to aid in this concentration. We already know the power of our minds. When we combine the Reiki energy and our intention, we create a powerful vehicle to aid the suffering of humankind.

117 Is there a mantra that I can use with Reiki to heal myself and others?

The use of mantras for healing is a wonderful extension of Reiki. Mantras are a series of syllables which hold frequencies or vibration. Many mantras activate specific frequencies of energy and correspond to specific archetypal energies. In Buddhism for example, there is the Mantra to evoke Medicine Buddha (the Buddha of Healing). When we say this mantra, it is not only an affirmation for healing it also evokes a series of frequencies which activate the bodies healing process.

The Mantra of Medicine Buddha can be used by anyone. In my book *'Reiki Healer – Lotus Press'*, a whole chapter is dedicated to this practice, however in short one may introduce the following as a means or aiding another with this powerfully healing mantra.

First imagine a blue transparent form of a Buddha manifesting above the afflicted part of the body you are treating. Think that this Buddha form represents all health and healing energies. As you repeat the mantra over and over in your mind, imagine that from the heart and pores of this Buddha's skin, luminous blue light issues forth. This blue light absorbs directly into the illness below your hands, purifying and healing any illness and disease. As you visualise this repeat the Medicine Buddha mantra as often as possible.

TAYATA OM BHEKHANDZE BHEKHANDZE MAHA BHEKHANDZE
BHEKHANDZE RANDZA SAMUNGATE SOHA

Pronounced:
Tay ya ta, Om, Beck hands zey, Beck hands zey, Ma Ha, Beck hands zey, Beck hands zey, Rand za, Sa, moon, gar tay, So ha.)

Once you feel as though the illness has abated through this practice, imagine that the blue Buddha form now dissolves into light and melts completely into the illness. We finish repeating the mantra and make the strong wish that this healing will continue to be of benefit for the person concerned. We also dedicate the merit of this practice for the benefit of all that lives.

118   Why does Reiki feel different from one treatment to the next on the same person?

This is usually an indication that the individual you are treating is assimilating the Reiki energy. When we are regularly working on an imbalance, a change of sensation is an indicator of a change in the person's overall vibratory level. In other words the person is regaining wellness. On the flip side, if we were working on someone and felt no change between sessions, then one could say that the effects were less dramatic. This is not to say that Reiki is not working, it may be an indication that further treatment is required. The Reiki energy also targets the primary cause of the imbalance. When we have a strong symptom that needs urgent attention, the Reiki energy will first attend to this outer symptom. Once this has been stabilized or cleared, the more subtle causes or layers are revealed. This often translates as new sensations or energy feedback during the treatment.

One could think of a change from one treatment to the next as a good sign, something is happening.

119 Does it matter which hand goes left or right when giving a treatment?

It makes little difference whether you are 'left' or 'right' handed, nor does it matter which hand is placed where. The Reiki energy is not governed by the left or right sides of the body. It is a non bi-polar energy and can therefore be administered equally on both or even on one side.

It is also worth noting that one hand is not stronger than the other, nor do we receive Reiki or give out the energy greater through the left or right hand. Reiki also doesn't need to be adjusted according to whether you are living in the northern or southern hemisphere.

Where some confusion arises with this point is the rules governing other system of healing. Other systems may use hands-on healing utilizing other energies and projecting this energy through the right hand, whilst receiving Chi or Prana though the left. This is a common method used for Pranic and some Chi systems of healing. Although we can incorporate these systems into Reiki, we are not dependant upon these rules when administering a Reiki treatment.

120 How important is posture when giving Reiki?

Posture is another point to consider. If we hold our body in a comfortable yet upright position we will assist the body's energy flow. Another thing we can do to assist energy flow is to gently rest your tongue on the roof of your mouth. To explain this further, our energy system operates to better or lesser degrees depending upon our posture. If we perform certain movements, generate certain hand gestures (Mudra) or perform certain postures, our own vital energy opens in new ways. This in turn creates openings within our energy system. The Reiki energy is then in union with our vital energy and can transfer in an effortless way as less obstacles to our energy pathways are present. One can think of this like a dry river bed which has been dammed. By generating a sound posture for healing, the dammed energy has a chance to flow. In this way we are working in union with our bodies' energy or 'Ki' and the Universal energy 'Rei' energy.

If on the other hand our posture is poor, the Reiki energy will still flow, however, our own 'Ki' or vital energy will be somewhat limited. This is why it is considered beneficial to have good posture whilst giving Reiki.

11

Giving Reiki to others
Part 3

121 What kind of pressure do I need to apply to my hands when giving Reiki to another?

Ideally when treating others little or no pressure is required. One should place their hands in such a way that they are lightly resting. It is important to be mindful not to place any undue pressure as this can be very disturbing for the person receiving. The best way to establish the correct pressure is to simply ask. Most forms of Reiki do not involve talking during the treatment, however once you have begun it is fine to ask your client if the pressure is ok. Some times people who are very sensitive to energies will find practitioners' hands to be quite heavy, in other cases the opposite may occur where the client who is more physical by nature may become irritated if the hands are too light. In any case the best way to get a feel for this is by asking.

Sometimes you will encounter new students who think they need to apply some kind of pressure to make the Reiki energy flow, or in other cases they may make their hands tremble or pull funny faces with too much concentration. The fact is Reiki is about doing very little. One often needs reminding that we are conduits of healing energy so it is best to allow, rather than force. Other times when giving Reiki to others, it may happen that you become so relaxed that you begin to lean and even 'doze off' by your client. Although I have only once ever experienced this on the receiving end, once was enough. Giving Reiki in a comfortable manner is as important as well as being mindful on every level of our being.

122 | Should I keep my fingers closed or open whilst giving Reiki to myself or others, and is there a difference in energy flow?

Generally Reiki is best transferred with the fingers relaxed and together. This focuses the Reiki energy in the area where the hands are in contact. Most of the time Reiki is a fingers closed affair as we generally wish to concentrate the energy to specific areas in need. If on the other hand you wish to use the Reiki energy to radiate or beam energy towards an area then spreading the fingers symbolizes this effect. With fingers spread open, the energy is much like a representation of the rays of the sun. The fingers spread out in this manner enable the healing energy to disperse in all directions to others.

In short, both approaches are valid and will bring about certain benefits, depending upon your desired effect.

123 | If I feel the need to move my hands above the body or back and forth during a treatment, should I do this?

As we begin to align more and more with Reiki energy, a merging occurs. This is a merging of our own innate awareness and the intelligence of the energy. Sometimes when we are working it may seem like the Reiki energy is guiding our hands and this can include working above the person's body or in other unusual ways. Should the feeling arise to do this, then it is fine to explore, one need only be mindful that is does not get out of hand. It is also important to be aware of the difference between intuitive impressions of Reiki guidance, and our Ego running off on some trip! One of the sure signs of Reiki Guidance is in the speed and spontaneity of the arising of impressions. Guidance in this way occurs without any prior thought processes. We simply feel guided and 'in flow'.

If we are working above the body, we need to indicate this to the person, so they know what to expect prior to treatment. Although this approach is not common it can serve as a benefit to your client and you may even be instrumental in co-creating an accelerated healing outcome.

124 How can I ground my energy after giving or receiving a Reiki treatment?

When we give Reiki to ourselves or another our mind enters a non-ordinary state of consciousness. Although we feel pleasant, we can often feel a little out of our bodies or light headed. This is fairly normal for people new to Reiki and tends to settle down with regular practice. If we do feel that we tend to drift off or have a problem grounding our energy after a session, then we should do one or a number of the following techniques to ground our body's energy.

Some of the following methods explore physical exercises, mental imagery and affirmations to keep your feet on the ground. Try some for yourself and see how quickly you come back to planet Earth.

1. **Eat more.** Although you may feel inclined to eat lightly when performing Reiki, if you are prone to lofty heights, intentionally eat more and heavier or bulky foods. This can assist in grounding your body and subsequently your mind. On the flip side, one should also be aware that overeating will have the effect of making you feel sleepy, so your common sense is important. Yang or grounding food include: eating meat (if you're so inclined), grains and vegetables which grow in or on the ground. These foods will pull your energies down and keep you focussed.

2. **Curl your toes.** Curling your toes, directs awareness to your feet. This method can be done during healing work or even during a Reiki treatment to assist in maintaining a grounded space. You simply curl your toes as if you are trying to pick up an object with your feet.

3. **Hara breathing.** Direct your breath deep into your lower belly. You may even imagine your breath is going down to your feet.

4. **Visualization techniques.** There are a variety of visualizations that can be applied. Here are just a few:

   A. Visualize your feet are spawning roots which anchor you to the earth's core, or that your feet extend beyond your physical body and lie deep in the earth.

   B. Visualize the power symbol from Second Degree Reiki and imagine this symbol spiralling down your legs and into the ground.

   C. Imagine you are wearing boots made of lead or that your feet are made from lead and are holding you heavy to the ground.

5. **Your environment.** If you are in a hot environment, wear lighter clothes. If your body is too hot, it is easy to associate this with sleep. Having fresh air and a well ventilated room, will keep your mind sharp and assist in maintaining a grounded state of consciousness. Be sure to have a blanket handy for your client as we do not wish them to get a chill.

6. **Physical Activity.** Having regular exercise will also assist in keeping you grounded. Whether this is a walk at the beach or in nature, gardening or rugged physical exercise, such as running, swimming, or working out, digging trenches or chopping wood. It's completely up to you. A good work out can really assist the body and mind in being present.

7. **Sexual Congress.** As well as being an excellent and most enjoyable thing to do the act of love making directly grounds the body's energies. This will not only improve one's mood, but will give the body balance, energy and grounding on a physical level.

8. **Using affirmations.** For example: *"I am present and grounded in the here and now."*

The best thing to do is to try these and see which ones work best for you. Being grounded in what you do and who you are is also important. If you tend to be 'off with the fairies' most of the time, then take a good look at how you can become more focussed on being present and engaged in the here and now.

125   Do I need to give Reiki for as long to a small child as I would with an adult?

As a general guide the best way to look at this is to think of the body as a container. An adult is a large container and a small child is a small container. Reiki is like pure water which we pour into the container. A simple equation would be smaller container, less water, therefore less time for the treatment. A larger body equals more water, meaning a longer time for the treatment. If you have the opportunity to work on small children or babies you will find that when they have had enough Reiki they will become agitated or no longer wish to be still. Remember, you cannot over do it and Reiki is always safe, so give Reiki until you feel that all that is required has been given, then there is no point in doing more. If a person is sick or depleted, no matter what size, more energy is often required, so the 'small container, big container' analogy is only a guide.

126 Why is it that during a Reiki seminar or in Reiki share groups, my energy feels strong, yet when I am alone, I do not feel as much?

This is a common question amongst new students and the answer is quite simple. The answer has to do with power-fields. A Power-field is the collective energy field of a group. This consists of the collective field of energy created by the students, the teacher, and the teacher's lineage. During a seminar and following Reiki share groups one is a part of this collective power-field and therefore the Reiki energy is not only coming through you, it is surrounding you. When we go home it is only ourself and the energy. As one is learning, it may take time to recognise this 'one on one relationship' and this is where self-healing and energy meditation practice becomes so important. One should also be aware that during the seminar, the Reiki attunements are opening you to a tremendous power. In time and with personal integration and practice it will make little difference whether you are in a group or alone, the power-field will be there in full force.

127 Is there a way to give healing at a distance at the beginner's level?

Traditionally in most Reiki circles, distant healing is only ever taught to students who have completed the Second Degree of Reiki. Distance healing utilizes Reiki symbols to affect the action of healing at a distance. However, when we examine exactly what distant healing is, we find the principles are similar throughout many healing traditions the world over.

The fact is, anyone can do distant healing and many of us do this already. One simple way to touch another is through wishes or prayer. Sincere strong wishes for another does work, it is just that we often do not recognise it.

In the chapter on distant healing we will explore many forms of distant healing but for the beginner a simple technique is presented here. This following method does not require the use of the Reiki symbols to create a bridge to the other person, yet the effect is much the same. This method enables an adequate connection for healing to be transferred.

1. With hands held at your heart centre in prayer position (Gassho Mudra), call in the person you wish to send healing to. Think of their name and where they are from in your mind. *"I am now calling in (person's name, from, etc...)"* do this 3 times.

2. Now imagine there is a blue sphere in space in front of you, the size of a person's body. The person concerned now manifests out of the blue sphere, materializing before you in space. (If you are sitting upright, they are a mirrored image to you, or if you are lying down, they are a mirror image of you on the ceiling). Imagine they are slightly transparent in appearance.

3. Place your palms facing them and now imagine the Reiki energy is flowing from your palms to them as blue light. This blue light is streaming into their body. The blue light completely heals and restores health and balance, do this for 5 minutes or as long as you feel is necessary.

4. Once this feels complete, imagine that they now turn into blue light and dissolve back into the sphere. Then the blue sphere dissolves into light.

5. Dedicate the merit by stating: *"May this healing activity just sent continue and grow. May this person be well and happy and free from suffering"*.

6. End the distant healing with your hands back in the prayer position at your heart centre and give thanks for the healing in your own way.

128 How important is Practice? If I don't practice will Reiki stop working?

Provided you have received the Reiki attunements by a qualified teacher, the energy will stay with you for the rest of your life. It can never be lost or hindered, even if you do not practice. Reiki is not affected by ones thoughts, emotions, beliefs, or your physical condition. The Reiki energy operates independently of these things. Having said this, practice is the most direct way to getting the most out of Reiki. With on-going practice you will greatly enhance your vital life-force energy. With this your health improves, and you grow spiritually.

Think of it like the muscles in your arm. When you have the attunements, you become aware of your muscles. In order to strengthen these, you need to use them, practice is like weight lifting. You cannot expect to see enormous results without daily practice. Just in the same way as you would not expect to become a strong weight lifter without daily training.

The teacher opens the door, it is your job to step through and see what lies inside.

To quote the Historical Buddha...

> It is you who must make the effort, the awakened only show the way. Who will liberate your own mind, if not yourself?
>
> V276 The Dhammapada

129 Is receiving a group Reiki treatment more powerful than from one person and how does this affect the outcomes?

The saying, *'many hands make light work'*, in some respects pertains to group healing. Although one can achieve excellent results with one practitioner facilitating healing, the more practitioners working in unison, the greater life force is bestowed.

In effect when there are many practitioners working on one individual the Reiki energy squares itself. Much in the same way as several streams filling a vessel, the time it takes to achieve this fullness is increased by the amount of Reiki streams entering the body at once.

We also need to consider the purity of the stream, in this case the experience and expertise of the Reiki practitioner. A Reiki practitioner with years of practice can often achieve a greater healing effect in the patient.

If the opportunity arises to receive a treatment from more than one person, seize the opportunity for it serves as a new experience in healing. This should in no way be a limitation, thinking that one person is kind of okay but ten people will make the world of difference. It is just different. One also needs to keep in mind that the Reiki energy will activate and heal what is necessary within you, be this with one, two or ten practitioners Reiki will give you what you need.

12

Reiki and its extended applications

130 Can I give myself Reiki to go to sleep and will Reiki keep on working when I fall asleep?

Reiki energy will still transfer regardless of your state of consciousness, so it makes little difference to the ability to use Reiki if you are asleep, awake or even distracted in your thoughts. The Reiki energy is activated by touch, so no matter what your state of consciousness, healing energy will still transmit when the hands are placed on or near the body.

Reiki is an excellent way to relax and this creates a natural pathway to sleep. If we can remember to place our hands on our own body when we go to bed, we evoke the healing energies to not only purify the day's impressions, but to also carry these positive energies into our sleep. In all the years that I have been teaching and treating others, I have seen the positive effects of Reiki on people who are suffering from Insomnia. Giving Reiki (particularly when we have a lot on our mind), enables a filing process for those things which we need, and do not need. When combined with meditation techniques Reiki can produce tremendous change and benefit.

If we are filled with too many impressions, it is important to give ourselves Reiki on the head positions as this enables the mental process to settle. Before practicing this method we call on the Reiki energy to remove all unnecessary impressions. We then think of the day and allow whichever impressions to arise. After several minutes you will often feel a change and drift into a deeply relaxing space. This process can be enhanced by utilizing the second symbol of Second Degree Reiki. This symbol assists in harmonizing thoughts and creates space in the mind.

Much in the same way as cleaning the hard drive on your computer, we wipe the unnecessary information from our minds and free up the hard drive for new programmes, hopefully virus free!

When you come to think about it we spend approximately one third of our lives sleeping, so Reiki whilst sleeping is a good habit to form. We can use this time for healing and this is especially good for busy people who find it difficult to find time in the day for regular formal practice. Having said this we should make every effort to practice with mindfulness during the day. The benefits of mindfulness practice over Reiki whilst sleeping are vast by comparison. Some regular practice in this manner enables steady spiritual progress and this is most important.

131   How could I use Reiki in a First Aid situation?

The first thing to remember when you are faced with a first aid situation is to apply first aid. If you do not have training in this area, you should take a short course as it may save your life or the life of another. Having followed the necessary stages of any First Aid situation, we can then consider the use of Reiki for First Aid. When treating someone, we can apply hands-on healing to assist the person in need. The idea is to work locally, if they have an injury, place your hands on or around the area of concern. Hands held just above when the injury is too painful to touch.

An example to illustrate this point happened during a Reiki workshop. A student whilst moving her car in the break came rushing back and didn't see the steel fuse box attached to the wall and ran headlong into it. Some time later she returned with a considerable lump protruding from her forehead. She was shaking, and in a lot of pain as well as having a mild concussion. Fortunately, we had a Doctor in the class and she quickly assessed the situation. She examined her head, and said that she would have serious bruising for many days and the lump would probably last for many hours, if not days. Seeing that there was little she could do except to give her some paracetamol for the pain, we Reiki practitioners set to work.

Wasting no time we laid her down as she was in shock and began hands-on healing. One practitioner had their hands slightly above the injury, one was working on the adrenal glands, and the third practitioner applied Reiki to her feet. As we were in the middle of teaching, we continued explaining some of the finer points of Reiki in regards to the situation at hand. Within a few short minutes, her shaking had subsided and she became relatively calm.

After just 30 minutes of hands-on healing, not only had her shock subsided, the lump had completely gone as well. Another 30 minutes later, she was up and walking around as if nothing had happened, much to the amazement of the other seminar participants and especially the Doctor. The next day our good Doctor's prognosis was also superseded as no bruising could be seen. This is but one example of hundreds of treatments which accelerate the normal rate of healing.

132 Is it advisable to give Reiki to someone who has been bitten or stung by something venomous?

As with any first aid situation, one follows the necessary steps as well as keeping the person calm and the limb (if bitten in this area) elevated and bound. One should also seek urgent medical assistance. Whilst waiting for additional help, one would certainly give Reiki to the sting or bite. Reiki would in no way speed up the effects of the poison, instead would assist the individual in remaining calm. Reiki will also pacify any associated swelling, inflammation or pain. One should give Reiki to the affected area for as long as possible until medical assistance has arrived. In the event you are the only person who can seek medical assistance the practitioner can be giving Reiki at a distance utilising an object of any description and corresponding this to the person concerned.

133 Can Reiki be used during pregnancy?

Receiving Reiki during pregnancy is a wonderful support for mother and baby. Regular hands-on healing benefits and can be used at any time during the term. I have personally treated several women at numerous stages of pregnancy with positive results. Regular hands-on healing offers comfort and relief from back pain, cramps, and swelling. It also acts as a relaxant and form of pain management during the onset of labour. When you are treating a pregnant woman, the thing to remember is that you are giving Reiki for two or in some cases three people (twins). What ever healing energy is transferred to the mother, the baby will receive as well. To recount a personal experience, I had the opportunity of giving Reiki to a very pregnant woman with twins. During the placement of hands-on on the mother's belly, both of the twins positioned themselves so that their heads were directly under my hands. Women who are pregnant will often have an aura of grace surrounding them. This glow is the life-force and protective energy assisting in the growth of the baby.

I have heard many success stories where families have gathered together with fellow Reiki friends to be present during the birth. Administering Reiki along side the paediatrician, or mid-wife assists the woman during the whole ordeal of labour. One should just be mindful, not to get in the way!

Although some doctors find this level of involvement challenging, many are open to it as the results are wonderful. In cases where this level of involvement is not possible, distance healing is another excellent alternative.

134 I heard you should not give Reiki to a pregnant woman, is this correct?

This is one of those Reiki myths. The idea is that Reiki could cause a woman to miscarry within the first three months of her term. This of course has no basis, Reiki cannot cause harm. Perhaps the real meaning for this caution was born out of the fear of litigation amongst Reiki practitioners. In the event that a Reiki practitioner was giving a woman Reiki who was in the early stages of her term, and during this time, the woman naturally had a miscarriage the blame could be placed upon the practitioner. This might be the reason for not giving treatments by some Reiki practitioners to women who are pregnant.

The Reiki energy is a safe energy and in no way could contribute to the loss of life. In fact the opposite is true, receiving regular Reiki treatments during pregnancy aids both mother and baby is numerous ways. The more Reiki is received during this sacred time, the better for all concerned.

This also goes for learning Reiki. Often students who are pregnant ask whether it will be safe for them to receive the attunements, thinking that these energy alignments may be too powerful and cause their unborn baby harm. I can say with some authority that I have trained dozens of pregnant women and the results have always been positive. One will encounter many limitations on the effects and use of Reiki; however, all but a few are created out of people's self-limiting beliefs and are not based on study and research.

135 Can Reiki be used to alleviate the symptoms of period pain?

Although I am not exactly qualified to comment, (being a man), I can say from the feedback I have heard from many women who have been treated for menstrual pain, that Reiki makes a noticeable difference. Many women swear by it and comment how Reiki makes every 28 day cycle more bearable. Not unlike a hot water bottle and aspirin all rolled into one, the use of Reiki for self-healing is excellent for period pain.

The method is simple, where it hurts, place the hands, and the results are often immediate.

Like any kind of body discomfort, by placing your hands on the area of concern will assist in bringing about relief from pain and discomfort. It all sounds like a headache tablet commercial, but in reality, it works just as well and in some cases even better.

Of course, if we find that our Reiki it not enough, we should seek alternative treatments or use Reiki in conjunction. It is not a case of throwing the baby out with the bath water one should imagine how they might incorporate Reiki into other forms of treatment, that way we are effectively taking the best from both worlds.

136 Can I energize food and water with the Reiki energy and what effect does it have?

The idea of blessing food and water is found throughout every major religion throughout time. So is this merely a belief based concept or is there any truth in the matter? In my experience it makes an enormous difference.

The following are some of the beneficial effects of blessing food and water:

1. Blessing food and water purifies toxins and impurities and can remove potentially harmful chemicals.

2. Blessing food and water, purifies negative karma in the form of anger or negativity associated with the cultivation and preparation of the food.
3. Blessing food and water will actually makes it taste better.
4. Blessing food and water is a direct way of placing Reiki into your body, via the food and water which has been energised.

Reiki is a direct way to enhance the positive effects of food and water, as well as removing the negative energies associated with it.

One should not abuse this by thinking that we can eat whatever we like in excess and leave it all up to Reiki to sort out. We need to make the right choices and utilise Reiki to benefit the process.

If you have received the Reiki attunements you can follow this simple exercise. We call this little experiment the 'Reiki taste test'. Take two glasses of ordinary non-filtered tap water. One glass is your control glass and the other is your test glass.

Leave your control glass to the side and place your hands around the glass you wish to charge with Reiki.

Now imagine there are streams of Reiki energy going into the glass. These manifest inside the water as tiny clear spheres of radiant clear light. Imagine that every drop of water corresponds to a drop or a sphere of light. Now imagine this light streams out in all directions until the whole glass is completely radiating Reiki energy. As you are imagining this, think that from your palms the Reiki energy is flowing into the glass, activating this purification process. Do this for 5 minutes or so.

If you have received the attunements for the Second Degree, you may draw the Power symbol over the glass (several times), and imagine that inside these spheres, the power symbol is radiating healing energy.

Now ask someone to taste the water from each glass. Be sure that they do not know which one is which. If you have done this correctly, the result that is often experienced is that the energised water tastes soft and smooth, where the ordinary tap water tastes like tap water. When you offer someone the taste test, be sure that they do not know which one has the energised water. This way we rule out any 'placebo' effect. Try this for yourself, the results are very surprising.

137 Does Reiki work on non-living objects, and can you recharge batteries with Reiki energy?

Reiki works on just about anything, be this people, pets, plants, or even everyday objects. These include: electrical equipment, cars, mobile phones, batteries and so on. One can actually recharge empty batteries to extend the battery life by following the example illustrated in the previous question for energising water. One simply holds the battery for 20 to 30 minutes and follows the same procedure. More often than not, the battery will be charged and further use can be made of it. Depending upon your ability, the battery will be charged in more or less time. In some cases, I have experienced batteries lasting longer than the usual lifespan. It also seems that the effects seem to differ depending upon the type of battery. For example, the length of time to charge and extend the batteries life differs from Lithium and re-chargeable batteries.

In the same way, one can have effective results with cars which have trouble starting, with home electrical equipment as well as your home computer[*].

When we consider that everything at the sub-atomic level is energy, we are merely incorporating the Reiki energy to increase and adjust the vibratory level. This in turn enhances the function. Have you noticed how things seem to flow better with love?

One can of course try these methods without being attuned to Reiki. If your intent is strong you will often have some effect. What makes the difference is the direct application of the Reiki energy, thus causing an energetic Reiki effect.

138 Is it possible to give Reiki to animals and can animals do Reiki or be attuned to the energy?

Animals of all kinds love Reiki and will often instinctively recognise Reiki practitioners. I will often have the disgruntled cat who hates everyone (except their owner) hop up on my knee for pats and healing.

---

[*] Although I cannot testify that Reiki will fix a broken or damaged item, it does seem to improve the function of many things. I can also say that many Reiki practitioners, including myself, energise the petrol going into the car at the gas station. It seems the car gets better mileage yet I have not tried to measure this in any proven way.

So it is wonderful to give Reiki to animals as well as being very beneficial. I know several vets who use Reiki as part of their daily practice. One can treat frightened and distressed animals, with excellent effects. Reiki is such a soothing and calming energy, a short treatment disguised as stroking or pats can be readily applied in most situations. In cases where the animal is injured or does not take kindly to close interaction, such as your pet spider, then beaming the Reiki energy at a distance or distance healing is an excellent alternative.

When giving Reiki to animals it is best to let the animal decide when they have received enough Reiki. When they have, they will generally get up and leave. Unlike most people, animals are less concerned in being polite so won't hang around just to please you.

As to whether an animal can be attuned to Reiki, remains a point of contention. In most cases, an attunement will act as a blessing. This contributes to the animals spiritual progress in future lives, so there is no harm in giving such a blessing. Of course one does not attune an animal in the same way as human beings, as their energy systems are quite different. As to whether an animal will be attuned and be able to give Reiki is another story. *Hands-on* healing, verses, *Paw-on* healing certainly stretches the imagination. However, I can relay a story of a cat named 'Pudding' whom I attuned to First Degree Reiki. At the time I was living at the local Buddha Dharma Centre, and seeing this cat turn up for morning meditation for the last 6 months, I figured I would give it a try. The attunements were given at a distance and after that, Pudding exhibited a tendency to place her paws on people who were visiting the centre for counselling and healing. As funny as it sounds, for Pudding this became a second vocation to hunting mice and sleeping. Many people actually reported a sense of energy flowing from her paws and she ended up living to a ripe old age.

139   What do I do if either my client or I experience sexual feelings during a treatment?

Because Reiki is vital energy, it can trigger sexual energy although it is not so common that sexual arousal presents itself during a Reiki treatment. Should sexual feelings arise, one should simply observe the thoughts and feelings without evaluation. If a mutual feeling of attraction is present, further treatments should cease and the feelings openly discussed so that the desired level of intimacy can be explored in a clear way. For some people there might already be an attraction between the practitioner and client and the Reiki energy brings this into awareness.

On the other hand, it the situation is one sided and the client is projecting their own agenda upon the practitioner, clear boundaries should be made immediately and it should be determined whether further treatments should be continued.

If it is the practitioner who has these feelings, then in no way should the practitioner take advantage of the therapeutic relationship.

140 Can Reiki heal issues of sexual trauma?

Reiki offers touch without a hidden agenda, so for those who have a history of sexual abuse they will often feel safe to release some of this trauma. When someone receives Reiki healing it may be the first time they have been touched in a loving way without any sexual undertone. In the area of sexual abuse, Reiki is a gentle and non-intrusive healing method for both mental and emotional healing.

Sexual abuse is a common problem amongst both men and women. Giving Reiki to our emotional pain can be an effective way to heal these issues whilst creating a space to be touched in a loving and nurturing way.

When giving a Reiki treatment for this specific purpose, the practitioner should in no way compromise the client's level of safety or boundaries. In any case, the hands should be placed above the area of abuse at a comfortable distance. This can be done by either working within the client's energy field, or by corresponding to a separate place on the body to the area of concern. In this way much of this trauma can be gently released.

If it is the case that your partner or spouse has some healing to do in this area, you as the practitioner, (with their permission) can place your hands directly on the genital area and simply allow the Reiki energy to heal and release. The suggested time frame is for at least 30 minutes, should this be comfortable for the person receiving.

In the case where the person has an emotional release, one should be there for the person and respectfully listen if they wish to share anything. Again it is not our place to offer advice or counsel them. Many times it is enough to be in the grace of the Reiki energy to gently release such issues. If your client begins to have a cathartic emotional release, the best thing to do is to ask them to take some deep breaths and even breathe with them. The breath is one of the most direct ways to release emotions in a safe and healing way.

Of course if latent emotions or memories are triggered which require deeper psychological assistance one should seek the guidance of a professional therapist or counsellor to aid the person in healing. It is not the role of the Reiki practitioner to put on the therapists hat unless licensed to do so.

141 Can Reiki be used between lovers to enhance intimacy?

Reiki between two loving partners is a wonderful way to enhance intimacy. Being 'hands-on' the uses are many.

One method for a deep and loving union between couples is a method called *Reiki Mawashi* or the *'heart meld'*. The method incorporates hands-on healing, synchronised breathing and visualization. This method can be done by anyone, whether you have been attuned to Reiki or not.

To begin, set the mood, dim the lights and create a space where you can relax and feel sensual. Sit opposite one other in such a manner that each can easily touch their lover's heart centre.

Now place your right hand on your lover's heart centre in the middle of their chest. They in turn place their right hand on your heart centre. Now with your left hand, place this over their right hand (which is on your heart centre) and they place their left hand over your right hand. In this way, their right hand is on your middle chest and your left hand is over their right hand, forming a circuit of energy. With the hands, palm over palm, maintain eye contact and begin to synchronise your breathing. When you breathe out, your lover should breathe in and when you breathe in, your lover should breathe out. Take slow, comfortable and gentle breaths. Visualise on your out breath that you are giving your lover the love from your heart and imagine this energy is transferring into their heart centre. As you breathe in, imagine that you are receiving your lover's heart essence from their heart to yours.

Keep your awareness on your lover and the love between you. Harmonizing in this way, you will soon fall into a deep union of loving affection which as the name describes, *melts* the hearts.

Once you have done this exercise, move your left hand from over your heart centre and place your hand over your lover's genitals. Your lover also holds or cups your genitals in return. You now have your right hand on their heart centre (as with the previous exercise) and your left hand is now holding your lover's genitals.

This time you direct your awareness and imagine you are breathing out your sexual healing energy through your genitals to your lover's genitals. Take turns in giving and receiving this love essence. On your in breath, imagine you are breathing in your lover's sexual essence from their genitals into yours and that this energy ascends to your heart centre. On the out breathe imagine you are giving your sexual essence from your genitals to theirs and up to their heart centre.

Do this for several minutes. By this point, you should feel intimately connected. Drink deeply from this sensual experience and the rest … I will leave that up to your imagination!

13

Reiki and Spirituality

142 What is Karma?

Karma can be roughly translated as 'activity'. One will often hear people say that person has good karma as they always seem to have good things, and people will think that when something bad happens that this person has bad karma. Although this rather simplistic view has some truth to it, in order to understand what is good and bad karma, it is best to explain how karma is actually created. In order for the full effects of karma to manifest, four factors must come together.

These four factors are:

1. Knowing the situation;
2. Thinking that one would like to do something;
3. To do it or have it done on your behalf, and
4. To be satisfied with the outcome.

To illustrate an example we could use killing a person. One must know it's a human being, one must wish to kill the person or arrange to have this done, the act of killing must take place and one must feel satisfied with the outcome. If all of these 4 factors come together the karmic imprint will be the strongest.

If, on the other hand, we are driving down the road one stormy night and we accidentally hit a person with our car and they die, then this is not strong karma as only one of the 4 factors came together. We did not set out to kill someone with our car, and although we know it's a human being and the act of killing took place, we feel badly that it took place.

Conversely, when it comes to good actions we can use the example of healing. We know in this situation that it is a human being in need. We make the strong wish to benefit the person, we perform the healing activity, and we are satisfied with our sincere efforts at the completion of the healing. So we can say that karma is a series of events and it is our relationship to it which determines whether it is good or bad.

Another example is the karma of speech. We would generally agree that if we lie, we will create trouble and this will in turn lead to the seeds of negative karma being sown. However, it all depends upon your motivation. Say you are sitting in a park you see a man running past you saying: *'help me! I am being chased by a gang who are going to kill me!'* as he runs off in one direction, a few moments later, the gang arrives and asks you in which direction did you see that guy run? Do you point in the direction he was running or in the opposite direction? Here the answer is the opposite direction for we save a life by lying. So it all depends upon our sincere motivation. Who is to say whether the man had done something right or wrong? All that matters is our ability to operate out of clarity in any given situation. That way we know how best to serve all concerned.

143 How do we create Karma?

Depending on your point of view, one can see this in many ways. From a Buddhist perspective our karmic situation is due to our previous actions in former lives. One of the principle things we need to know is that through all of our thoughts, words and actions, we are sowing the seeds for our future karma. All the things we do, say, and think create our future. Be these positive or negative.

We can also say that the things that occur right now in our lives are due to old karmas ripening from former lives. When we truly grasp the idea that right now we are creating our future self by all the things we do, say, and think, we recognise the importance of right actions, right speech and right mindfulness in this moment.

When we perform wrong actions it is much like taking poison. The problem with most people is that they do not recognise this and continue to perpetuate their negative karma. Due to negative karmas ripening now, many people operate out of this ignorance; and continue to harm themselves and others, thereby perpetuating even more negative karma in the future.

In the Dharma, the lives of beings are often described by four categories.

The first are those who have harmed in the past and use this negativity to create even more harm in the present. This creates even more harm in the future and thus the wheel of sorrow continues to spin.

The second class of beings are those who have harmed in the past, yet in this life sow what they can to create benefit in this life. They may exhibit many good qualities, yet still their lives are filled with misfortune. People say, *"why does this person have so many problems, she is so kind to others, why do bad things happen to good people?"*

The reason for this is due to their previous negative karma ripening in this life.

The third class of beings are those who accumulated good karma in former lives, yet in this life they squander this good karma to create harm and misfortune for others. This is the person who is corrupt and causes harm yet appears to have good fortune in this life. Their previous good karma is quickly spent and in the future (or future lives), their seeds germinate in misfortune.

The fourth class of beings are those who performed many good actions and have accumulated many good impressions from former lives. In this life they use this good karma to perpetuate even more benefit for others. Thus they sow even more good karma which will assist them in the future.

Many people who are involved in or who are attracted to spiritual matters and healing are usually situated somewhere in the second and fourth classes. One can do much to counter negative seeds through the activity of benefiting others. Healing others and helping them to help themselves is one of the best ways to purify negative seeds from ripening.

144 Are people who do Reiki in this life, doing this because they were healers in former lives?

If we can accept the notion of reincarnation, then we can say that our mind stream has had many lifetimes. Who we are now is a sum total of all those previous lives. We carry this information which culminates in the expression of who we are.

To realise this we need only look at our own lives to recognise that the person who we feel the best connection to, the occupation we find ourselves in, the person who we find the hardest to like, have all played a role in our previous lives.

To say that people who are doing Reiki now, have done it before, may, or may not be, but if one feels a strong connection to the Reiki path, then it would be safe to say that that person has certainly been exposed to healing or spiritual practice from former lives.

All of the impressions from former lives as well as our connections to the people we meet in this life, are all contributing factors. It is these factors which are karmic and pull us towards the right connections with people in this life. All this determines certain vocations, our relationships as well as our likes and dislikes. Have you ever met someone and within a matter of minutes they seem close and familiar like an old friend?

In a sense we are all continuing were we left off last time. Much like a television series, this life is the next part of the last episode. The choice is whether our next episode is a drama or an adventure. Based on our previous actions we draw the appropriate resources and people to match this experience. In this way we continue the process in this life.

Now some people have a karmic pre-disposition for music, whilst others have a karmic pre-disposition for science, whilst others still have a strong karmic pull towards healing work and spiritual activity. When it comes to healing, the more lives we can touch, the greater good we can spread throughout the world. If we can be a living example, we can teach others how to heal themselves.

145 If a client has an illness due to past karma and it is their karmic path to experience their illness, by attempting to heal that person are we interfering with that process?

Reiki is a fabulous tool for healing others and as Reiki energy is for the highest good of all concerned, our will does not interfere with another's karmic path. Who are we to determine whether or not our healing is to interfere with their karmic process? It may be the individual's karma to meet the practitioner who will assist them in healing. In the case where the person does not appear to heal in the desired manner, then it may also be that the individual's karma is already determined. In short, we can alter an individual's karma through our actions, yet this will occur as part of their own collective karma. With this in mind, one should always do the best to one's ability. For the for-ordained karmic outcome cannot be assumed by the practitioner. Who are we to say that this is or is not a karmic path of another?

Unless you happened to be genuinely enlightened, it is wise not to pass judgement. We can have all kinds of speculation, yet this will lead us no closer to the truth. In any healing work, it is our role to be of service in a meaningful way. We should never withhold our ability to benefit others.

An example of this might be with a terminally ill diagnosed patient. We approach the treatment with the sincere desire to benefit, yet without the expectation that we will cure or reverse their illness or situation. When it comes down to it, even if we have the greatest healing tool known to humankind, if it is the karmic destiny of another to pass forward, then there is little say we have in the matter. If on the other hand, it is the karmic path of our patient to meet and receive healing from ourselves and by that integration, a cure is effected, (being part of that person's karma) then this too is the person's karmic path.

We should view all situations with a sense of openness and possibility. If we can do this and remain optimistic, yet objective and un-attached to the outcome, we can be of clear benefit to the individual.

146 Do I need to change my diet or become a vegetarian to practice Reiki?

This is a matter for each individual to choose. Although some Reiki teachers may advocate a specific diet, (especially prior to a Reiki class) the system itself does not dictate whether one should be vegetarian or otherwise. The core essence of Reiki is to discover healing through mindfulness, compassion and living a balanced and middle way. The emphasis in Reiki is to become reacquainted with your body and this means listening to what your body requires. If you know certain foods benefit you whilst others do not, the teachings ask that you serve your body rather than being a servant of your body. Once you understand this principle and act upon it, you will naturally come to a place where you know what is suitable for yourself in any given moment. Reiki brings you back into balance.

One way to illustrate this is with the Taoist symbol of Yin and Yang. We probably have all seen this symbol at some time or other. The symbol represents perfect unity and balance. The Yin-Yang symbol (also known as the symbol of the Tao) compromises of two distinct parts, the male energy and the female energy. Yang or male energy can only truly function with the cooperation of its female counterpart. Likewise, the female energy is only truly in harmony when it is working in consort with its male counterpart. This is represented in the symbol of a small blank circle representing the male energy within the female energy and a small white circle representing the female energy within the male energy. Each contains a part of the other, they are joined in union. It becomes a manifestation of wisdom and action, skill and means, intertwined as one.

As to the moral issue of eating meat, one also needs to consider this for oneself. There is always a karmic result to our actions. In many spiritual communities it is considered taboo to practice a spiritual path and eat meat. Yet in other spiritual systems it is considered to be alright if one is not directly involved in the act of killing. For example, it is considered wrong to order the execution of an animal or fish, say in a Chinese restaurant. Others refrain from fishing or other related acts where a being will directly suffer or die due to our actions, whilst others will simply refrain from any actions which will cause the harm of sentient beings.

Kalu Rinpoche*, one of Tibet's greatest Buddhist masters, would often stop along country roads and yell out mantras to livestock and other animals that might otherwise be killed on the roads. I know another Rinpoche who made the decision not to drive as the act of driving would result in many insects being killed on the windscreen.

The fact is we cannot help but harm and kill. Each time we walk or breathe, we inevitably kill organisms, insects and other little creatures. The point is our motivation or desire to kill or harm. It is our motivation which results in the primary cause of Karma.

---

* Rinpoche is the titled given to high Lama's in the Tibetan Buddhist tradition and denotes a teacher of superior accomplishment who is believed to be the rebirth or emanation of a previous highly-developed Buddhist practitioner. It literally means 'precious one'.

147 What are some of the long term abilities which arise from long term Reiki practice?

Some of the possible side effects of on-going practice may include becoming a better person. If we participate in regular practice, many of our ego trips and much of excess baggage can be purified. But this must include a dedicated commitment to our own personal growth and healing. Of course each of us has varying degrees of this baggage to deal with and one should use whichever methods achieve this end. It is quite advisable to clean up your own life before advising others on how their lives should be. If this means taking therapy, or taking personal growth training, then so be it. Few people come into this life with a clean slate. There are so many ways to cut through our illusions these days and the practice of Reiki is one which generates merit as it is an act of service and generosity. Through service and sincere motivation to help others (as opposed to wanting to be seen as helping others), we slowly but surely subdue our pride. Through healing others we also generate a lot of positive merit and this in turn is very helpful in purifying our negative karma.

The more we practice the more we become like the energy. Reiki is love, Reiki is harmony, and Reiki brings balance. As we think, so we are; as we act, so we create. You must be as you would become, so the more you wear the smiling face of Reiki, the more it sticks. This is about being authentic, honest and real, but also about becoming more. With further practice one becomes a peaceful person and less inclined to participate in the leading roles of life's dramas.

Many people who dedicate themselves to ongoing practice also become more attuned to subtle energy. This can manifest in many different ways such as a heightened sense of awareness and intuition. Many will also generate greater clairvoyance and will generally be more able to recognise the best way in order to benefit others and situations. At an ultimate level one's mind becomes like a mirror. One takes things less personally and one sees all beings as having the same potential for awakening. All this of course takes time but the more we practice and generate the sincere wish to benefit others the more we walk a steadfast road to liberation.

14

Second Degree Questions

How does one determine whether one is ready to learn the Second Degree?

The decision to learn Second Degree is an individual one. Some practitioners like to learn this level very soon after the First Degree, whilst others may spend years waiting before taking this next step. If one was to learn Reiki formally in the Japanese Reiki Society, a student may take as long as ten years before learning the Second Degree, however their system is based on various mini levels called proficiency levels throughout the First Degree. In the west it seems things are a little different. Our society is geared around instant results. We have instant coffee, shake and bake cakes, microwave dinners, and even instant spiritual attainment, (for the right price). For many, learning quickly with the least amount of personal effort is unfortunately how many spiritually material minds tick. However, there are many kinds of students and a teacher needs to be able to identify which kind of student is which, so that they can guide them in a better course of practice.

Some students take to Reiki with so much ease that they find that they can progress directly and attain the results which exhibit a high level of proficiency. I think it would be safe to say that in every spiritual practice there are those who excel and those who struggle. Just as there are those students who are inherently lazy and those who work diligently with devotion.

One of the important things to consider before taking the Second Degree is a review of what you have learnt from the previous level. A great way to test your Reiki proficiency is to review a First Degree seminar. This is an invaluable experience as revisiting what you have already studied surprisingly opens your awareness to the things which we missed the first time around. Every class is different because the people attending are so different. So a review is always highly recommended. Another simple exercise one can do is to ask oneself some of the following questions?

Do I know and use the material from the First Degree?
What is my level of understanding of these methods?
Do I regularly utilise the self-healing techniques?
How sincere is my motivation for learning the Second Degree?

At *The International Institute for Reiki Training* we offer our students an accreditation process where they are required to have completed a minimum amount of clinical practice hours. Once these hours have been completed they may proceed to the Second Degree. This ensures that we create a framework for practitioners to work within, which enables the practitioner to practice in a supervised environment as well as to log the necessary amount of practice hours. This commitment to experiential practice is crucial to gaining a base level of practice.

149   Are Reiki practitioners required to have insurance in order to practice?

If you are working in a clinic or in conjunction with other health professionals, public liability cover will be a requirement. For general Reiki practice, many Reiki practitioners are opting to take out Public Liability insurance. As far is this being a requirement depends upon the laws which govern the practice of Reiki in your country. If you are unsure of these laws, contact your local government, insurance agency or ministry of fair trading.

If you are in a situation where you are offering healing work from your home, practice room, or office, then it is wise to have your own public liability cover. For example, if your client falls down your stairs and wants to sue you, or in the unlikely circumstance where your client claims that your Reiki treatment had a detrimental effect upon their health then cover is recommended. The truth of the matter is when we look at how non-invasive Reiki is, as well as Reiki' lack of contra-indications, the risk factor is practically non-existent.

Provided we conduct our session in an ethical and respectful manner, by following a suitable code of conduct, the chances of actually harming a client with Reiki healing is very remote to say the least. In over 12 years of practice, I have not had one instance where my insurance was claimed on, even for something minor, yet I choose to have cover, just in case the situation ever arose.

Many insurance agencies now offer cover for Reiki practitioners and other complementary therapists. Our Reiki Institute also offers access to cover via our membership base. If you would like to know more, visit our Reiki website at: www.reikitraining.com.au or our Complementary Therapists website at: www.iict.com.au

150 Can someone who has learnt a different Reiki style pick up a new Reiki style from a different teacher or does one need to review previous levels?

If a student has learnt Reiki from another teacher and wishes to learn Second Degree Reiki from another teacher, then providing the new teacher has the same Reiki lineage and same attunement procedures as the former teacher, then this is not a problem. Continuity is assured because both teachers are using similar methods. If, on the other hand, one teacher offers different attunement procedures to the other, which can even occur within the same style, then most teachers of Reiki recommend a review of the previous level and re-attunement in their Reiki lineage and methods.

The truth of the matter is that there is tremendous diversity in the teaching of Reiki and as a result, in most cases one requires re-attunement in previous levels before proceeding. Just as one could say: *Tae Kwon Do* and *Kung Fu* are both Martial Arts, one could not assume they were the same in methodology. So it is to a lesser extent with the various styles of Reiki.

Each teacher also brings their own unique approach to Reiki. It is not uncommon to learn something completely new when re-sitting a previous level with another teacher. If, on your journey, you have the good fortune of finding a good teacher who embodies Reiki, and has a clear transmission, then it is better to continue to learn from such a teacher. It is of little use changing from one Reiki teacher to the next, if you have already met an excellent teacher who carries a genuine transmission.

In the case where you are unsatisfied with your teacher and his or her ability and your intuition tells you, *'there must be more to this'*, then seek a teacher who can give you the methods you seek. It may take time to find a suitable teacher, and you may need to travel, as well as make personal efforts, but if you find a teacher who can give you the tradition in its purest form, it is well worth the effort.

It is your responsibility to seek a teacher who can show you the way. It is our duty to pursue the spiritual path, and no one can do it for you. A teacher only opens the door, and it is you who must enter and walk through.

151 Should I wait until I am completely healed before healing others?

In the teachings of the Buddha, he described there are four types of beings in this world. There are those who look after themselves and ignore the welfare of others. There are those who look after others and ignore their own welfare. There are those who neglect their own as well as others welfare and those who look after both themselves as well as others welfare.

So it depends upon which if these four you predominantly operate from. Some feel that it is vitally important to heal them self or that they are somehow unworthy to offer healing to others. This might be because they have so many perceived problems that they will somehow transfer their agenda upon the very people they are trying to help. On the other side there are those who neglect their own self-healing and overly focus on healing others, saying: *"Oh, I don't need any healing, I'm fine"*, or they think: *"I am not worthy of being healed"*. So they help others to avoid dealing with their own problems. One needs to strike a balance between healing others and healing oneself.

152 Can Reiki be used to heal the environment?

Reiki is an excellent medium for healing environments, old impressions as well as stagnant lower vibrational energy. By engaging in practices which transfer healing energies into an environment one can have a positive and lasting effect.

There are several methods for healing environments, some of which are already in print, detailed in my first book, *Reiki Healer*. However, to expand on these practices, the following method is a simple way which any practitioner or non-practitioner can use to bring a positive influence into their home, work place or favourite space.

The Blue Sphere Meditation.

Sit or stand in the middle of the room, or an area which seems to be the focal point of the room or space which requires clearing.

Now imagine you are a mighty tree. Feel that your feet are deep in the earth, your roots stable and secure. Your arms are the branches. They are strong and stretch outwards into the sky.

Imagine you are this strong tree and stand with your arms out to the sides of your body. Spread your fingers outwards to radiate in all directions.

Once you have imagined this in your mind, bring your hands together at your heart centre and breathe easily and gently.

Now imagine outside yourself in all directions are spheres of blue light, some are big and some are small. These blue spheres represent the unlimited power and potential of Reiki. Imagine countless spheres now pulsate and radiate like stars in the nights sky. In your mind, think to yourself, *"I now invite the unlimited power, purification and healing of Reiki into me now"*. With this, the spheres of blue light now merge with your body, filling it with blue light. Take your time to imagine these lights filling your body until it is completely full. You are now the embodiment of the blue lights and your tree is even stronger than ever.

Now as you inhale, these blue lights begin to stir inside you. When you exhale, these blue lights begin to expand outside your body, filling the space around. Continue to inhale, stirring more blue light and exhaling which further expands the blue lights around you. With each exhalation your sphere grows bigger and bigger, much like someone blowing up a blue balloon.

As the sphere touches any negativity, it is instantly transformed into the blue light. Continue doing this until the entire environment is completely filled.

This ends the meditation.

153 Can Reiki assist with healing relationships?

Reiki can be beneficial in healing relationships but before I explain this it is best to first establish the correct view of relating. When we fall in Love we see the divinity in another. This divinity is simply a reflection of our own divinity.

After sometime, we get to know the person better and this freshness which so inspired us begins to fall away and the newness disappears. We trap the spontaneity and freshness further, by clinging to what we had. When we hold on, we cling, and the very thing we want, slips through our fingers.

The way to maintain this freshness is then to let go of our fixed views of how the other person should be. When emotional love fades from view, we are met with our attachment. Here we need to watch our minds, for our desires and wants are selfish in nature. If we lose sight of this our selfish nature translates to seeing the faults in ourselves as being the faults in the other. This in turn creates even more ups and downs, and round we go on the bumpy ride of relationships.

At this point we might think that this person is not beneficial for us and we start to think about escaping. In truth, we want to escape ourselves. It becomes so uncomfortable to face this fact that our only escape is to find a new shining face. For many this becomes a pattern. We have not met ourselves, so we attract the same type of person, different face, presenting again the same kinds of issues. We might ask ourselves: *"What is it with all these guys or girls?"* You might ask yourself: *"What is it with me?"*

To free up love, we need to drop our selfish ways. Instead of seeking to fill our needs we should seek to see how we might benefit our partner. How might we serve them in a meaningful way?

Of course, commonsense plays a part and one needs to recognise whether there is enough raw material left once all the glamour wears off. It is said that half of all relationship problems can be solved by simply finding a compatible partner. If you find someone who you can get along with, who will be your friend and your lover, who shares common goals and interests, then you are half way there. You have found a foundation upon which you can build.

When problems arise, it is usually to do with either harmful and selfish actions, like betraying trust, telling lies, getting caught, or treating the other in a way which is completely in discord with the way in which they would wish to be treated.

Other problems arise out of the small stuff. Caught in the illusion of our divine partner, we make a big drama out of the little things. The Indian Master, Shantideva said: *"One person harms another out of ignorance; someone else becomes angry out of ignorance. What makes the one blameless and the other an object of blame?"* and this: *"There is nothing whatsoever that is not made easy through familiarity. Practice patience with small difficulties, and thus gradually become patient with greater challenges".*

In other words, when we cause a problem in a relationship, it has two sides, we may have upset our partner due to a wrong action, or we may in our own minds have done nothing to harm the other, yet by acting as a trigger to the others process, what is seemed by us as ripples actually creates waves. So it makes sense to first give up harmful actions and replace these with acts of generosity and kindness and to be ever watchful of our minds.

Of course, if we have an abusive partner who has no desire to grow, then one may need to consider what is best for us. We should be in the business of cultivating Love. Not loveless relationships because we are afraid of meeting ourselves if we are single. A relationship is about creating the openness of experience and to be open to seeing the other as an aspect of your own unfolding. In this way we can create a fertile ground for love.

Reiki can also support this process. When we feel there is a rift in our relationship or that of another, we can utilize the harmonizing effect of Reiki to bring balance into the situation. Essentially we plug back into love and the flow of the Divine.

An effective means is to send Reiki to the situation. Note, this does not necessarily mean the two individuals involved, rather the energy pattern which is actually created as a result of the discord. This way we take out the fuel which is driving the fire.

By healing and dissolving the clouds of disharmony between two people, one removes the object of the discord. Then one may work directly with each individual's personal problems and projections in order to remove the root cause of the problem.

The following is a general guide to healing disharmony between two people.

1. Firstly, identify the situation. What is the root cause of this issue in me? What is the perceived issue in my partner?
2. Once you have established this send Reiki to the situation. For example: *"I am now sending Reiki healing to bring harmony between myself and my partner"*.
3. Send healing energy with the intention of healing and dissolving the energy surrounding the conflict.
4. Once this is completed, now call in the root cause of your issue with the other party.
5. Send distant healing to this root cause, remember you may not know precisely what this is. The Reiki energy will go to the cause. Remember, you are simply the medium for this process to transfer.
6. Once this is completed, call in the root cause of your partner's issue. Again, you may not know what the pattern is, just sends the healing to affect a beneficial outcome for all concerned.
7. Once you have completed the three healing directions, repeat the process each day until you see a positive change in the situation. Chances are you will, however, one must also be active in the outer world and be prepared to practice patience and tolerance to meet the healing energies of Reiki with your own desire for change. This incudes listening to what your partner has to say. In this way we can be more effective and support the business of Love. Isn't this what it's all about anyway?

154 | What general guidelines are recommended for setting up a Reiki practice?

The first thing I would recommend is that the practitioner should have achieved a sound understanding and experience of Reiki. This takes the form of adequate practice and personal integration of the teachings. Many practitioner's who have learnt Reiki, realise that it is beneficial to have gained some practical hands-on experience and have therefore spent a considerable amount of time, before taking on a Reiki practice. So it is important to determine whether you are ready in the first place. It becomes a question of readiness and at the same time, one does need to throw oneself in the deep end to see if the fruits of their practice will keep them afloat financially.

Some practitioners are too eager for their own good, with little experience to see them through. In this case, the practitioner who has this level of striving can be better tempered through further practice. On the other hand we find the practitioner who has been practicing for years yet avoids the step of setting up a practice through lack of self worth. Here this type of person is better served with a proverbial spiritual kick in the pants to get things rolling. Even angels need a push to get flying!

When it comes to the practicalities of setting up the practice, one should certainly work within the guidelines of proper moral and ethical codes as prescribed by most health care professionals.

The other thing is to find a suitable venue for your Reiki practice. One requires a place where relative peace and quiet can be maintained so as to conduct your treatments in a relaxing and harmonious way. This also includes who your neighbours will be and the general energy of the venue. One also needs to consider how one will advertise oneself. It is vitally important that the phone actually rings. There is no point in having a Reiki practice if you do not have any clients. One needs to determine a rate for ones time and energy so there is fair value placed on the services you give. You should also consider having the appropriate equipment, including a treatment table for your healing sessions.

You might also consider doing a short course on people skills and basic counselling. Always remember to work within the bounds of your ability and never prescribe, nor diagnose, a client's condition unless licensed to do so. Once you have these important points in order, you can step out into the community to serve and benefit others with the sacred healing of Reiki.

155 Can Reiki be used to protect me from harmful circumstances?

Generally speaking, regular use of Reiki will generally begin to generate greater spiritual strength. This then translates into a protective energy field.

The more you become accustomed to the use and practice of Reiki; you naturally begin to radiate this healing energy around yourself and in your life. One of the best forms of protection is a positive attitude. If you are inclined to be the *'glass half empty'* type of person verses the *'glass half full'*, by actually changing your view this can do much to create a change.

156 How can I use Reiki to heal emotions like anger?

Anger is one of those emotions which many people experience. The trick is not to engage in or give your anger a chance. In the teachings of the Buddha, anger is said to be one of the most dangerous emotions. The great Indian Buddhist master, Shantideva wrote: *"There is no negativity as strong as anger and no spiritual practice as important as the discipline of restraint from it. The person who understands that anger is the real enemy and works with persistence to overcome it, and who does not identify enemies as external, finds happiness in this life and in whatever follows thereafter".*

It says in the teachings of the Buddha: *"Let go of Anger, let go of Pride, when you are bound by nothing, you cannot fall prey to sorrow."* and this:, *"Transform your anger with kindness, your meanness with generosity, your lies with truth."* and this: *"You too will die some day, knowing this, how can you quarrel?"*

The teachings are so simple, yet when we are faced with adversity it is all too easy to ignite angers' flames.

The effects of anger have also been proven to be directly related to the chemical activity of the brain. When we get angry, we actually produce harmful chemicals which then circulate throughout our entire body. In effect, we are literally poisoning our bodies every time we give into anger. Anger also damages our mental and emotional selves. Although we somehow feel justified by giving our protagonist a piece of our mind, all we are really doing is creating further harm to ourselves.

Expressing and getting into our anger has been a recent trend in modern psychology, and it seems that much of these intensive processes do much to create more problems than they solve. Although modern psychology has much to offer, processes which actually encourage the expression of anger, have little to do with health, healing and cultivating a well mind. Anger is a friend we cannot afford to keep.

If we look at how anger actually serves us, we need not look further than the nightly news. The world is full of suffering from the actions of intolerance, anger and self-righteousness. When we get all fired up by something that has happened to us it is entirely our choice how we choose to view the situation. It is our choice. If a problem proves too difficult, you have a choice to remove yourself from the situation. The next approach is to cultivate compassion and the third approach is to transform harm into wisdom.

One of the most profound methods in healing anger is through the practice of loving kindness. The following suggestions might also be helpful in cooling the flames of anger.

a. If someone has harmed you, give them a gift from the heart, something useful for them that will be appreciated by them.

b. Observe your mind, and create some distance. When you observe that anger is rising, talk to yourself: *"Here is anger arising in my mind. It wasn't there before it won't be there in the future, so how does it serve me now?"*

c. Generate compassion. Think to yourself, *"This person gives me an opportunity to heal my anger. This is really an aspect of my own process. This kind friend has given me a gift. I should thank them for giving me an opportunity to examine my mind and emotions."*

d. For those who are really confused and cause us harm, we can think: *"So and so, has much confusion and is obviously operating from his/her own conditioned experiences, I see him/her once a week and I feel upset for only a few minutes. This poor person however, spends 24 hours with themselves. I should feel compassion for their sorry existence."*

e. Wellness and Happiness Practice. Begin with all the people you love. Think: *"May my wife be well and happy, may my friend be well and happy, etc…"* Generating the sincere heart of good will, move to people you have a neutral feeling about. *"May my teacher be well and happy, may the bus driver be well and happy, etc…"* Then move to the people who cause you sorrow, *"May so and so be well and happy, etc…"* The thing is to do this exercise with a sincere heart.

f. Radiate love and kindness: Imagine all the people you love dearly standing behind you. Now imagine all the people who cause you sorrow in front of you. Imagine you have a radiant sphere of purifying light inside your chest. Now imagine this light (Reiki energy) goes out and touches all the ones you love. Now imagine all the purifying lights go out to all the people who cause you sorrow. These purifying lights completely purify all your negative karmic bonds and there are no more debts to pay.

Of course with any of these exercises it is not enough to think: *"May all beings be well and happy…..except for you!"* It is necessary to cultivate love and compassion for everyone, like one big (functioning) family.

Then we find there is no room for anger and only understanding and compassion will grow.

157 How do I know if a session has worked if no visible signs are apparent?

It is not always the case that you will give a person a Reiki treatment and they will jump off the table singing out: *"I'm healed!"* As much as we would like this to happen with every session this is not the usual experience. When no visible response comes back from your client, one should not think that they have failed. The thing to remember is that Reiki often has a delayed effect and that it may take some time to integrate. Much like throwing a stone in the centre of a lake, the ripples spread out over the surface of the pond.

Another reason when a person shows no sign of progress, maybe your client is contributing to the cause of their problems between sessions.

We need to look at the problem from a whole of life perspective. At other times someone will come to you for a treatment and the problem they presented with is not cured, however, something else is. Lastly we should recognise that Reiki is not the only way of healing, so one should utilize other avenues. If the person would benefit from seeing a naturopath or allopathic physician, then one should make recommendations.

158 Can Reiki be used as the sole method of treatment for serious illness?

Reiki should never be considered the sole form of treatment of an illness. Although Reiki can certainly assist in the healing of many things, Reiki should be applied in conjunction with traditional allopathic medicine, as well as other complementary natural therapies, such as Chinese Medicine and Naturopathy.

If a Reiki practitioner knows the client is in need of urgent medical care, it is completely irresponsible and reprehensible not to refer that person to a qualified medical practitioner. Reiki blends wonderfully with almost any form of health care. It should be seen as a complementary adjunct to western medicine. There is tremendous merit in both. At the end of the day if one generates a state of wellbeing and health as a result of western medicine, or alternative therapies, ultimately it is the end result which matters the most.

159 Can one energise Western Medicine with Reiki energy?

Reiki has a beneficial effect when applied to medication. Before taking your medication, place the pills or tonic between your hands and energize them with Reiki. One can also utilize the Reiki symbols in conjunction with this to promote the positive qualities of the medication and to reduce the possible side effects.

The same goes for any herbal supplements, or other alternative medicines, such as Chinese herbs, Homeopathy, Flower Essences, or Aromatherapy. The application of Reiki is a wonderful way to enhance the therapeutic effect of most medicines.

15

Reiki Symbols Questions

160 What are the Reiki symbols?

The Reiki symbols are comprised of four forms, three of which are traditionally given at the Second Degree level and the fourth, given at the Third Degree. Two of these symbols are modified Japanese Kanji, the other two are more abstract and have their origins in Taoism, Shinto and Buddhism.

The Reiki symbols act as keys to opening specific pathways or fields of energy. They are also used during most Reiki attunement procedures and activate the practitioner's Reiki ability. Each symbol has specific meanings and direct applications in healing. When used in the correct fashion, they enable the Reiki practitioner to direct these fields of energy which in turn have a specific vibrational effect upon the energy fields of anyone receiving them.

161 Why are symbols used in Reiki?

Before we look at why we have symbols in Reiki, we need to first look at the symbology and the role it plays in the lives of human beings. We are in effect surrounded by symbols constantly; though the media, though our daily interactions with one another and through our dreams.

Symbols are everywhere and are an essential tool for communication, verbally; mentally; and energetically.

When we use the Reiki symbols, these, unlike mundane symbols, communicate a specific frequency and a doorway into a field of energy.

Each symbol in Reiki contains within it an outer, inner, and secret meaning. This means that each symbol has a specific function, a specific vibration, and a specific effect on the whole of our being.

The Reiki symbols act as a vehicle for the Reiki energy to travel, or if you like the symbols act as energetic keys which unlock certain pathways of energy for the practitioner. And likewise when used during a Reiki treatment can assist with the application of healing energy in specific ways.

The symbols used in the Reiki attunements, (if used correctly) awaken a lasting pathway to Reiki energy. Through further initiation, the symbols enable others to carry the lineage forward so that even more people can continue in a similar fashion.

162 How are the Reiki symbols used in healing?

The most common way the Reiki symbols are used in healing are by either, signing, visualizing or infusing these into the recipient's energy field or Chakras. This in turn effects a change in the energy field's resonance. All imbalances, be these physical, mental, or emotional, manifest in the energy field. These translate as specific vibrations which are resonating at a specific rate. The application of the Reiki symbols is a very direct way to increase the amount of higher vibrational energy within the energy field. When this is facilitated, the lower resonance of the illness or mental/emotional imbalance is raised. This in turn lessens the symptoms and a state of balance and harmony results. The application of hands-on healing will also achieve the same result. The difference being, the direct application of the Reiki symbols enables this more efficiently. One therefore increases the amount of life force energy in such a way as to restore balance. As the Reiki symbols are direct pathways to this healing energy, their use in Reiki is most effective.

163 Can anyone use the Reiki symbols for healing without initiation into Reiki?

In order for the Reiki symbols to work, each symbol requires the appropriate Reiki attunement by a qualified Reiki teacher. The teacher through the method of attunement bestows the symbols activation and thereby the ability for it to be activated within the student. As a result, the initiated student then has the energetic permission to use the symbols. It is much like having a light bulb which is in a light socket. The switch which lights the bulb is the attunement given by the initiating instructor.

164 Can I use the Reiki symbols to protect myself?

The Reiki symbols are a high resonance field of energy. When one signs a symbol they create a high frequency of energy and light. Once this energy has been created or brought to life via the practitioner, it can be used to increase one's energy field. This in turn acts as a direct way to protect ones energy field from lower vibrational energy.

Therefore, one of the best ways to achieve this end is to sign a large symbol in the air in front of you and to step into it. As a result your energy field and the symbols energy field merge. In this way the resonance of your energy field is dramatically increased, which as a result serves as a protective field surrounding your body.

165 What are the names of the Reiki symbols?

The names of the Reiki symbols are the specific mantras which are an integral part of the symbols energy field. This energy field is created each time a symbol is signed. For the full energy effect, it is necessary to have the physical symbol form and its mantra in order to create the living energy field. The person signing the symbol must also have received the initiation into the symbols for the Second Degree. Some secrecy still surrounds revealing the names of the Reiki symbols, yet without the attunement into this level, it is not like the power of each symbol is somehow lessened. As I have mentioned, one requires the Reiki attunement in the Second Degree from a qualified teacher in order to bestow the symbols power. By way of this introduction the names given in the Second Degree symbols are as follows.

The first symbol is called '*Choku Rei*'. This symbol is referred to as the '*Power*' symbol as it is generally said to activate the Reiki energy when signed.

The second symbol is called '*Sei Heki*'. This symbol is referred to as the symbol of '*Harmony*' as it is said to activate the vibration of harmony into any area of discord.

The third symbol is called '*Honsha Ze Shonen*'. This symbol is referred to as the '*Connection*' symbol as it is said to activate a connection to others in distant healing. This symbol is also known as '*The Bridge*', as it bridges the Reiki healing energy from one space and time to another.

166 Can you tell me some of the Power symbol uses in Reiki?

The Choku Rei is a Reiki symbol which activates and increases the Reiki energy. Much in the same way as focusing energy onto a target, this symbol focuses the Reiki energy into one point which has a stabilizing, purifying, and sealing effect. Choku Rei will increase power, is a quick activator, increases strength, brings in Reiki energy, seals in Reiki energy, and as a result dispels negative energy. As well as these uses some of the other ways this symbol is used includes:

- The Choku Rei is a great accelerator, which directs and focuses energy wherever used. Repeating the symbol increases the amount of Universal energy.
- When signing the symbol always draw the symbol once and say the Kotodama (mantra) three times.
- The Power symbol can be used by itself, but can also be used in conjunction with other symbols, activating and enhancing their qualities. This symbol is also usually used at the end of a sequence of symbols to increase power.
- The Power symbol can also be drawn onto the palms of the hands before commencing a Reiki treatment for either oneself or others.
- The symbol is also often used once the treatment is completed. The symbol is then drawn over the body of the recipient to seal in the Reiki energy.
- The Choku Rei can be sent in distant healing to revitalize any person, thing or situation.
- The Choku Rei can also be used to set up sacred space in a room or used to clear the energy of a room when drawn in each direction. This symbol will purify and bless your home, work place, car and the space surrounding your physical body.

- This symbol can be used to release negative energy; in people, places, objects, and even situations.
- It can be drawn over food or water to enhance the nutritional value and to purify negative contaminates.
- It can boost the healing properties and reduce the possible side effects of medications as well as boost and empower the effectiveness of flower essences, essential oils, gem elixirs etc…
- It can be drawn over crystals, and amulets to enhance positive energies and protection.
- It can be drawn over doorways or windows, so that anyone who enters is cleansed of negative energy.
- This symbol, like the other Reiki symbols can be placed physically behind pictures, under your pillow, in your car, in medications etc… enhancing the energy fields of the places or objects concerned.
- This symbol can be used to bring light to someone who is dying to assist them when passing forward.
- If one feels out of balance, one can draw the Power symbol over ones crown Chakra, then bring it down to the base Chakra, to re-energize oneself.

Overall the Choku Rei improves physical and material energy in the body and mind. It brings all of the Reiki energy into one point and awakens the flow of Universal energy where the symbol is directed.

167 Can you tell me more of the Harmony symbol uses in Reiki?

The Harmony symbol *(Sei Heki)* restores psychological, mental, and emotional balance and brings deep healing. This symbol also helps to remove bad habits when applied in specific ways on a mental level. The Sei Heki promotes self-growth by increasing sensitivity and acceptance. In addition to this the Se Heki also assists in resolving all kinds of mental disorders. It opens the subconscious, balances left and right brain, and enhances memory. As well as these uses some of the other ways this symbol is used includes:

- It is used to align the body by balancing the upper four Chakras for mental, emotional and spiritual harmony. It activates the Divinity within and awakens and purifies the body's energy.

- This symbol like the others is drawn once and one says the Kotodama (mantra) three times.
- This symbol is often used second when used with other symbols or first when used for mental/emotional balancing.
- The Harmony symbol opens the mind and heals the mind/body connection through the subconscious. It acts as a key or doorway to access information on a clairvoyant level.
- It assists with the gentle release of negative emotions and trauma by bringing them to the surface.
- This symbol can also be used for protection and boundaries in healing, by placing the symbol around an area of the body, the whole person, place or object.
- Sei Heki activates the highest potential within a situation or being, bringing harmony and resolve.
- Sei Heki is also used for releasing attachments to past issues, by cutting energetic ties, as well as being used for forgiveness and letting go.

Over all the Sei Heki is mainly used to restore psychological and emotional balance. It assists in relieving mental and emotional pain, negative feelings, and many psychological imbalances.

168 Can you tell me more of the Connection symbol uses in Reiki?

The Connection symbol (Honsha Ze Shonen) connects to target healing through time and space, bringing deep healing and transformation. The Connection symbol is mostly used for distance healing. As well as these uses some of the other ways this symbol is used includes:

- This symbol acts as a vehicle to direct healing energy in absent healing.
- This symbols Kotodama (mantra) is always said three times when drawn.
- The Connection symbol is usually used in conjunction with the other two symbols and is usually drawn first in these sequences.
- Honsha Ze Shonen can be used to direct healing energy to the past. For example, to negative situations, past traumas, previous illness, injury, or even to specific times in ones childhood or infancy.

- The Connection symbol can be used in the present moment to direct healing to oneself or another. It can be used to send healing to current situations which need resolve and resolution. It can also be used to centre oneself or another, and to create the support for the mind to remain still in the present moment.
- Honsha Ze Shonen can be directed into the future. This may include directing healing energy to future appointments, places, or situations. One can actually direct healing energy to take effect at a later date or place.
- This symbol can be used on the body to direct the Reiki energy to places where the hands are not in contact. It also enables the practitioner to be in several places at once, either physically or energetically to direct healing into the present and past simultaneously.

Overall the Honsha Ze Shonen is used for Distant Healing but it is also useful in healing karmic situations which cause harm and prevent the individual from moving forward.

169   Why are the Reiki symbols shrouded in secrecy?

Amongst certain Reiki schools, the secrecy surrounding the Reiki symbols is significant. One of the common practices initiated by Mrs. Takata and later enforced by members of the Reiki Alliance was at the end of a Second Degree seminar (where the symbols were revealed) each student was required to burn the visual depictions of the Reiki symbols at the end of a Reiki Seminar. One would view the symbols and then commit these to memory. As I recall during my own Second Degree Reiki class, I too participated in this practice. At the time I found this to be a rather odd practice as we as human beings are prone to forgetfulness. Sure enough, one year later in a Reiki review seminar when I was asked to draw a visual depiction of the Reiki symbols, some were grossly inaccurate to the original forms.

The practice of burning symbols at the end of seminars has today largely been removed as it was causing more and more confusion and differences in the Reiki system than maintaining tradition. It is also evident that Usui and several of his direct students supported the use of written manuals and did not enforce the memorising of information to the degree of preventing the written form.

Today in the world where everything is being published online or in books, many depictions of the Reiki symbols and even the Reiki attunements can be viewed by the general public. The Reiki symbols by themselves do not awaken a practitioner's pathway to the Reiki energy. One always requires a living transmission from a qualified teacher.

Where some confusion arises with the Reiki symbols, some teachers believe the visual depictions themselves will awaken the Reiki ability however, it is clear that the Reiki symbols require the necessary attunements from a qualified teacher, only then is the ability transferred to the student and their Reiki ability switched on. In this way viewing the Reiki symbols by the uninitiated makes little difference without the necessary attunements.

170 What are non-traditional Reiki symbols?

Just as there are non-traditional styles of Reiki, so it is with symbols. The previously mentioned symbols of Second Degree as well as the Fourth Reiki symbol which is traditionally bestowed at the Third Degree make up the traditional Reiki symbols of Usui Reiki.

Other symbols which have been introduced into Reiki can generally be said to be non-traditional symbols. Non-traditional Reiki symbols are utilised by many Reiki styles and offer ways for the practitioner to direct the Reiki energy. In a similar way to archetypes which embody certain attributes, many non-traditional Reiki symbols can represent attributes for additional ways of directing the Reiki Energy.

Over the years, as many new Reiki styles have emerged, new symbols have either been created or borrowed from other systems of healing, esoteric traditions or religions to act as tools for working with the Reiki energy.

Many symbols can be used as tools for healing, provided they carry a history or can be conveyed via transmission to the practitioner.

Just as one requires initiation into the traditional Reiki symbols, in most cases one requires the accompanying empowerment for the symbols if presented within a Reiki seminar of a particular style. However, in some cases, depending upon which Reiki style, this may or may not be the case. The question is then how effective are non-traditional symbols and do they work in the same way for all?

171 Are non-traditional Reiki symbols as effective as the traditional ones?

This question can be answered as a yes, no, or maybe depending upon several factors. It depends on the symbol, how it was bestowed, the ability of the one who bestows it and the way in which the practitioner utilises it. Without citing any of the previous scenarios, in general many non-traditional Reiki symbols are effective in harnessing the Reiki energy in specific ways. One must recognise that symbols represent qualities. For example, a symbol might be used for grounding energy. The practitioner is shown the symbol, and its meaning, and then they may or may not receive an attunement for the symbol. Armed with this understanding one might utilise it in healing to assist their client to ground their energy at the end of a treatment. In order for this to work, several other factors are at play. The symbol is much like a lens. When the practitioner utilises this lens the Reiki energy manifests as a specific vibration. This vibration has all the qualities of grounding. When the practitioner signs the symbol and repeats the symbols Kotodama (mantra) this vibration activates the symbols accompanying energy field. This field or frequency is directed via the practitioner to the one who receives it. Thus a field effect is formed and this has a direct effect on the one receiving it. This may sound rather complicated, however, it is only the numerous factors which accompany healing work which presents such complexity.

In order to be effective with symbols, one need only utilise these to determine their level of effectiveness. The results will be evident if the symbols attributed manifest in the person you are treating.

172 Can the Reiki symbols increase the amount of Reiki energy transferred in healing?

In most cases the Reiki symbols will form an increase in the amount of Reiki energy transferred. For example, the Choku Rei is a symbol which serves this specific function. In general this symbol assists the practitioner in maintaining their level of focus and concentration. When focus is present, the awareness of the practitioner is more open for the transference of Reiki energy. To use the analogy of a magnifying glass and the sun, focus and concentration with the use of symbols, directs the rays of the sun (Reiki energy) and therefore increases the amount of the energy being bestowed. The other thing to consider is the quality and power of the magnifying glass. This represents the level of the practitioners experience and how much of a clear channel they are for Reiki. The more one practices Reiki, the more this channel becomes clear. So this too plays a part.

One can receive all the empowerments in the world, as well as all the symbols, but if one does not practice, little benefit will ensue.

173   How important is it to have the correct renderings of the Reiki symbols?

Although some Reiki teachers would not agree, a near enough rendering of the Reiki symbols is sufficient for results. In an ideal situation we would all possess Usui's original hand writing of the Reiki symbols, yet for almost all of us, this is not the case. The thing to remember is that although there are many variations of the traditional Reiki symbols, these variations work. The primary reason for this is due to the Divine Intelligence of Reiki. If we as human beings meet the symbols with a desired effect in mind, the energy itself meets us half way and creates the rest.

If you compare the Reiki symbols from one Reiki teacher to the next, you will see a slight change here and a slight change there. In much the same way that people's handwriting styles vary, so it is the same with the way the Reiki symbols are drawn.

Although it is ideal to emulate original renderings of the Reiki symbols, it is not essential. Provided you do not remove or add new strokes or change the Kotodama (mantra), then you will still achieve sound results.

174   Do the Reiki symbols have a power of their own, or is it the Practitioner's faith in them which activates the power?

The Reiki symbols are a combination of the practitioner's ability to summon them as well as the Divine Intelligence of Reiki to empower them. If the Reiki symbols were only based on the practitioner's faith, the ability to use them would not be consistent for all. The fact is that when a practitioner who is empowered to use the symbols creates the symbol by signing it, a living energy field is created. This is also the case for Reiki attunements. If the Reiki symbols had no inherent power of their own, then the Reiki attunements would not work every time for those who receive them. So it is a combination of both faith and the inherent power of Reiki energy which activate the symbols power.

175 Can the Reiki symbols lose their power if you show them to someone who is not initiated into the Second Degree?

The Reiki symbols cannot lose their power, however one can lose ones faith in them through doubt and superstition. Ideally it is best to reveal the Reiki symbols to those who are learning the second level as they serve little purpose for those who are uninitiated. I know of many Second Degree practitioners who like to graffiti the Reiki symbols on the sole of their shoes. Some readily write them on cards and put them in their wallets. Some practitioners do the same by placing them behind pictures on the walls. If someone sees a rendering of the Reiki symbols then no matter. One can simply say that it is a symbol for good luck, or a symbol for healing. You never know, it might just be the thing which gets them interested in learning Reiki.

16

Distant Healing

176 What is Distant healing?

Distant Healing is the ability to send Reiki energy to someone who is not physically present. Depending upon the method, one can send Reiki healing at a distance, either by the use of the Reiki symbols, Mudra (hand gestures), visualization, or pure intention. In many cases, one uses a combination of these to achieve a healing outcome. We see that in many religious systems the use of distant healing is common. Be this through prayer, good wishes or the use of an effigy to represent a person, distant healing can have a powerful effect to heal and create positive change. We generally find that distant healing is often accompanied by ritual and symbol. This ritual process in Reiki terms involves a connection to the person via the Honsha Ze Shonen symbol, and sending Reiki either through a proxy of some kind to represent the person we wish to heal.

In the case where the practitioner utilises the law of correspondence, an object effectively becomes the person concerned. A common example is to use an object which has a head, body, arms and legs, and what could be more convenient than a teddy bear? Once a connection is made, the practitioner places their hands on the object and states that their hands correspond to the same place on the person they wish to heal. For example, the practitioner may state: *"My left hand now corresponds to (the person concerned) heart and my right hand corresponds to (the person concerned) forehead"*. The practitioner then places their hands in these same positions on the proxy and administers Reiki as if the person were present. What is often surprising for those who do this for the first time, is that the normal sensations which accompany hands-on healing, are the same with distant healing. So where one might feel heat emanating from their palms during a hands-on healing treatment, the same experience will be felt on the humble teddy bear.

177   Is there more than one way to do distant healing?

Although a common method is via an effigy to represent the person we wish to heal, there are many alternatives. Other methods utilize a photograph where the practitioner places their hands on the photo and directs the healing energies to the person concerned. In other cases, the healer can utilise a familiar object of the person, such as their watch, a piece of jewellery or even a piece of the recipients clothing, hair or finger nail. All of these items can be a focal point for the Reiki energy.

Other methods include the practitioner utilising their entire body to represent the individual concerned, however this method is not advisable for the seriously sick or emotionally and mentally disturbed patients as ones personal boundaries cannot be so clearly defined. In such cases this method can be challenging, so it is advisable not to use this version for the seriously ill. The general rule of thumb with this method is that if you would feel comfortable giving the person concerned a hug then this approach is a wonderful way to connect. However, if you would not, then better to use another distant healing method so as to better maintain a clearly defined boundary.

Other practices involve creative visualization where the person is imagined as in between their hands or in space before them. Other practices use rituals and symbolic processes or Mudra (hand gestures) to evoke healing energies for remote healing.

Whichever method you choose or have been taught, the practice is most beneficial and can dramatically increase the healing outcome of the person or situation concerned.

178   If I take my hands off the effigy or if my concentration is disturbed, will this stop the distant healing?

When using the method of an effigy to represent the individual, then concentration is useful in the beginning when calling in the mind stream of the person concerned. In this way we are more able to sense the connection. Once a connection is made, the healing energies flow without ones conscious awareness. Much in the same way that our minds can be otherwise pre-occupied whilst facilitating hands-on healing, distance healing is very similar. This is why the method of an effigy is popular as it does not require extended periods of concentration to bring about positive effects.

Using the method of an effigy as the basis for distant healing, the connection is maintained by the hands in physical contact with the effigy. If contact is broken, whereby both hands are no longer in contact, then the mind-stream of the individual is also removed. This is in no way harmful to the recipient the healing energy just stops flowing.

In the case of transferring healing via a 'visualization' process then concentration is a must. Our ability to hold concentrated awareness becomes the point of focus for the energy to transfer. A focal point is essential for healing of any kind, be this the persons physical body in hands-on healing, or distant healing, we need to anchor the Reiki energy to something.

179 Do I need to use the same effigy for distant healing?

If one is giving regular distant healing, then using the same object to represent the individual is most useful. The reason for this is by using the same object for distant healing, the object itself becomes attuned to the positive healing. Each time we give Reiki via an effigy, Reiki energy is transferred to the person concerned, yet the object itself accumulates more and more healing energies with each use. With regular and prolonged use, the effigy becomes a healing vessel and one can simply pick up the object and be affected by its healing field.

This acts in a similar manner to ritual objects, like prayer beads or religious icons. If objects like this are held with devotion and focused attention they become manifestations of benefit to all who come in contact with them.

In order to maintain and build up these good energies it is advisable to use the same effigy for the same purpose of distant healing. It is not necessary to have a new effigy for each person, yet keep the item in a way to support the integrity of the practice and out of the way of those who might hold and play with it.

The thing is that we can use just about anything as a proxy. In my first book, 'Reiki Healer', there is a chapter of how one can use crystals as a proxy for distant healing. Crystals hold and store energies and these can be used as excellent ways to focus healing energies for distant healing. One can use just about anything as a proxy. I know a friend who smokes, so he uses his cigarette lighter as a proxy. I know another lady who likes to do all of her distant healing on the train, utilising her handbag as a proxy. It all seems to work, just as well as more conventional methods.

180 Can distant healing be harmful if the person receiving it has not given their consent?

This is an often asked question as the issue of permission for sending distant healing has a diverse array of views and concerns. One should know that Reiki energy whether it is administered hands-on or sent at a distance is always a beneficial practice and in no way will it ever harm an individual. This is also the case where the person concerned has not formally requested to receive it. The view we should hold is to offer healing to those in need. If we happen upon a situation where we know someone who could really benefit from our healing activities yet they are not very open to things of a spiritual nature (due to their own views or the views of others), we should still offer to treat the person. This is not to say that we should begin a sacred crusade to heal everyone, but to withhold our healing abilities with the view that we will somehow interfere with the person's path is erroneous.

We cannot ask an animal that is sick if they formally would like to receive distant healing; nor can we ask a baby or someone that we see on the evening news. The truth of the matter is that when we send distant healing we are sending a loving and healing energy. This energy comes from the source of Divinity; it is pure and intelligently guided.

Ideally, it is good to offer healing with the persons consent, yet it is not essential. In this case it is best to set up a time for the transference of distant healing so that the person on the receiving end can treat it much like they would a hands-on healing treatment. In this situation the practitioner determines when the healing will transfer and for how long. The recipient then creates the space for that allotted time to lie down and be quiet for 10 or 20 minutes to receive the healing with awareness. If one conducts distant healing in this way it is extraordinary the kind of correlations which occur. It is also a good way for those who are more sceptical of such things to prove the benefits to themselves. This is often an assignment that we set for our students who train through our Institute in the Second Degree when distant healing is taught. On the Saturday evening of the seminar, we pre-arrange times for distant healing between workshop participants. That night each person performs a distant healing at the requested time. The recipient lies down for a period of 20 minutes and notices what they feel during the treatment. The person who is facilitating the distant healing also takes notes of areas where they sensed the energy flowing. The following morning we share our experiences and in most cases, more than 80% of participants receive almost 100% confirmation that the experiment worked. When we perform distant healing, our ability to perceive areas of imbalance and other psychic information is greatly increased as we are intimately connected to the recipient's energy field.

181 Is distant healing stronger than hands-on healing?

It is my experience that both forms of healing are equally valid. One is not necessarily better than another. It is really a question of which form of healing is possible in any given situation. Distant healing is a wonderful way to offer healing to situations, people, animals as well as many other applications, and is a direct way to heal others without the usual physical barrier of the body. On a pure energy level we work on the energetic imbalance and thereby directly affect a healing outcome. On the flip side, when we have a person present and place our hands-on, the person is there and knows and feels the healing energy transferring. Hands-on healing conveys healing through touch and one can experience the healing qualities of being nurtured and nourished.

182 Can I give Reiki to someone who has died?

You can, although once the body dies you are better off giving healing and comfort to those loved ones grieving the departed. In my first book, 'Reiki Healer', I give specific instructions on how to assist a person who has died with Reiki, however in short the best thing you can do is give them distant healing to assist them through the intermediary state between this life and the one that follows.

One can call in the person's mind stream in much the same way when giving distant healing. It is important to call in the mind stream and not the body as you will find that the mind no longer resides there. When you have their mind stream between your hands and have transferred this thought form to an external effigy, send distant healing to them each day until you can no longer obtain a connection. When a connection can no longer be made, this is a clear indication that their mind stream has moved on. This means that the attachment to their former life is complete and they have in most cases taken re-birth with new parents. The best time to facilitate a distant healing on the one who has died is on the seventh week anniversary date of their death. It is at this time that their mind stream is the closest to this realm. This process can be continued up to a period of seven weeks, however during this time all but a few would have moved on.

For many, the study of death and dying might seem a somewhat macabre subject but for some religious systems, in particular Tibetan Buddhism, a wealth of information on this topic can be found. If you wish to know more of the death and dying process please read Sogyal Rinpoche's book, *The Tibetan Book of Living and Dying.* This book gives a user friendly view of the whole process.

183 Can I send Reiki energy into the future?

Reiki can be sent into the future to create a positive outcome. For example, if we had an important job interview next week, we could send distant healing to the interview in general, or to the person who would be conducting the interview. Alternatively we could send a distant healing to ourselves, so that we are calm, intelligible, and clear.

When we send healing into the future, for a desired effect, we really create a space for others to interact with their energy, even if they are unaware of this happening. Sending Reiki into a future situation can do much to create a positive space and in that way we are more inclined to bring out our best. Have you ever noticed that when you are in a loving, peaceful and happy environment, it is harder to maintain sorrow? Yet when you are in an angry, confrontational and violent environment, it is harder to maintain joy? When we send Reiki healing to another for a future event or place we create an environment which assists in a positive outcome. People naturally respond well to this as we are creating a welcoming and wholesome energy which brings good will for all concerned.

Some examples of how we might use Reiki distant healing for future events include the following: For an important interview, for a future goal, for a future exam, for a future presentation, for a future meeting, a trip, a court case, or anything you can conceive where you would benefit being supported by the Reiki energy. The possibilities are endless.

184 Can I send Reiki energy into the past to heal my present issues?

For past issues we can send healing to specific times we recall which presently cause difficulty in our lives. Here we send healing energy to the root cause of the current problem. In some cases we may not know when this was, yet by sending Reiki into the past to heal the cause, can create a positive shift in our current situation. One can send distant healing to a time in the past, like an injury for example. When we send to this time the Reiki energy can assist in removing the trauma associated with that experience. In this way we gain a new perspective for now and this experience flows into the present, which in turn can make changes in our current experience.

For those of us who wish to heal the relationship with our inner child or for those who wish to connect with this playful aspect of our minds, sending Reiki to ourselves as children is a wonderful extension to distant healing. The process is the same as distant healing the only difference being is the 'calling in' stage. Here we state that it is to ourselves at a particular age that we wish to send the distant healing.

One can think of distant healing as a 'time machine' where one can send Reiki to heal the past and create the future you desire. It is important to note that it is not necessary to re-experience something unpleasant from our past in order to heal it. Sending Reiki to our past is not meant to be a form of re-birthing or some form of regression therapy. We do not have to dredge up the past, nor do we need to know all the details or re-live these sometimes unpleasant experiences. The Reiki energy only needs a point of focus and the rest is left up to Reiki to heal.

185 Can I send healing to every year of my life and how do I do this?

The whole life distant healing procedure is a direct way to purify many of the obstacles which we have accumulated throughout our life. It is also a direct way to heal many mental and emotional issues which affect us in our adult lives.

To get the most out of the procedure it is best to give oneself the healing procedure each successive day until it is completed. The procedure is undertaken on a daily basis with one distant healing per day in the following manner.

The first step is to send a distant healing to your conception. This is the time where your mother's egg and father's sperm united. At this point your mind stream entered and your life began. The second step is to send a distant healing to the gestation period in your mother's womb. The third step is to send a distant healing to your birth*.

(*Note one should spend extra time for this distant healing.)

The fourth step is to send a distant healing to yourself from birth to your first birthday, then the day from your first birthday to your second birthday, and so on. Continue in this way until you reach your current age. In effect, each time you send a distant healing, you send Reiki for one whole year of your life.

If, for example, you are 57 years old, then the whole process will take 60 days, including your three distant healings up to your actual birth.

How the Reiki energy heals is by targeting the most significant dates within each year. Each successive healing has an accumulated effect, so each day you increase the power of each session. By the time you reach your current age, you have cleared many things within you and will be no doubt feeling clearer within yourself.

An additional practice during this process is to actively forgive anyone during each year and to give thanks for what you have received. A prayer which can be said during each session might go along the following lines: *"I now fully and freely forgive everyone who caused me sorrow at age (state the particular age you are working on) I also forgive myself for any harm I may have caused others. I am now free and all karmic debts are now cleared. Having thus been purified, I now give thanks for the lessons learnt and the understanding I can now bring to myself and others. May all beings be well and happy and free from sorrow"* (Repeat three times).

186 Can I send Reiki healing to more than one person at a time?

There are several ways to send distant healing to more than one person at the same time. The following are two ways to effectively achieve this end:

Method 1   The Reiki Box
Collect all the names of all the people who require healing. These can be placed on separate pieces of paper, including the person's name, their date of birth and where they live. If possible it is also great to have a photograph of the person concerned and to write their name on the back of the photo. Any of these previously mentioned points gives the Reiki energy a point of focus for the distant healing.

Now take each photo or piece of paper for the individuals concerned and sign the three Reiki symbols over the photographs.

These are usually drawn in the following order:

Connection symbol, Harmony/Protection symbol, Power symbol.

Once each photo or piece of paper has been signed with the three symbols, place these in a box. The box itself need not be large or elaborate, however due care should be taken when acquiring a box for distant healing work. It is preferable to choose a box which is made from natural substances, such as wood, bone, shell, stone, silver, gold or crystal.

Once each individual has been called into the healing space, place your hands over the box and send distant healing in the usual manner. Effectively, each person will receive a full treatment at a distance. The thing is that this technique saves loads of time.

Method 2   The Reiki Board
This method works in a similar fashion to the previous exercise. Where it differs is with the use of a pin-up board and the method of directing distant Reiki.

Place a large board in front of you at a comfortable distance. Hold each photo or piece of paper with the persons' details and sign the three Reiki symbols over each one.

Once all of the photos or papers have been signed, place these up on the board; set them out in rows or in some other fashion which feels right for you.

Now place your hands out in front of you, and create a triangle with your fingers by joining your thumbs and index fingers. Your other fingers should radiate outwards with your palms facing away from you. Radiate your fingers outwards and imagine Reiki energy beaming to all the photos on the board in front of you.

Continue to send like this for as long as you feel necessary and close in the usual manner.

187   How can I use distant healing to manifest my goals?

Distant healing is one very direct and useful way to assist with achieving goals, both short term and long term. The following method is one of many ways to make things happen with Reiki.

1. Write on a piece of paper what it is that you wish to achieve. Then write down all of the perceived obstacles which may prevent you from achieving your desired goal. Include obstacles both inner, (meaning your own thoughts and conditioning around receiving your desired goal) as well as all outer influences.
2. Now write a list of the things you need to do to achieve this goal. These are the small steps which lead to your desired outcome.
3. Now write down what you are prepared to sacrifice (give back to the Universe) to achieve this goal.
4. Now write, in a few lines, a definitive statement which summarises your goal as if it is already manifested in the world. For example: *"I now choose to manifest (state your goal, by (insert a time frame, date, etc). This or something better manifests now for the highest good of all concerned."*
5. Now take all of your notes and place these between your hands. Sign the three symbols as per the distant healing method. Whilst sending healing energy to your goal, imagine yourself in the future as if it has already manifested.
Concentrate only on the desired outcome and imagine yourself in that future outcome for the whole distant healing.
6. Once you feel enough healing energies have been sent, close in the usual manner and once again repeat your definitive statement.

Continue doing this daily and within a short period of time you will start to see results. The reason that we focus on the outcome as if it has already occurred is so that we can allow the Reiki energy to create a pathway to the very thing we wish to co-create. As we focus on the future, so we become it.

188 Can I work on more than one issue at a time when giving a distant healing?

Ideally it is better to give one distant healing for one issue at a time. The reason for this is that if we focus all of our intention in one place we give the Reiki energy a focal point to generate the desired result. If we call in several things which require healing or goals which we wish to manifest, it weakens the focal point. As with all Reiki methods, the more we can bring to them, the more focused intent is created. You cannot cut through a massive stone with a feather, just as in the same way that you will not achieve results in a speedy fashion if you divide your focus. It is much like having a target to focus upon. If you go for a drive and do not have a destination, you could end up anywhere, least of all where you need to be. When we focus on one thing at a time, it is like our destination is in full view. Then all we need to do is follow the steps and the Reiki energy will take us to our destination. In this case the healing outcome we desire which is in harmony with the benefit of all concerned.

17

Reiki Mastery

189 Is everyone who is a Reiki Master a teacher of Reiki?

No, essentially there are differences. A practitioner may have taken Reiki training in the Third Degree, yet have not taken the step to actually teach others. In other cases they may have even finished a one or two year apprenticeship under their chosen Reiki Instructor and although they may have been given the title Reiki Master, this does not automatically qualify them to teach Reiki. Some Reiki styles even include an additional Reiki attunement to confer the ability to pass on the Reiki system. In other cases, some Reiki students simply wish to participate in the third level of training for personal reasons, and to increase their inner experience of the Reiki energy. This is why some Reiki schools offer a Fourth Degree to make the distinction between Reiki Masters and those who are teachers.

190 What is a Reiki Master Teacher?

This is a term which often describes someone who has actually finished their teacher training in the Third Degree and is teaching students of their own. A *'Master Teacher'* does not necessarily mean the teacher is somehow better to hold a higher status. More so, it is an indication that they are active in passing on the Reiki tradition and initiating others into the Reiki lineage. In other cases, the title 'Master Teacher', can describe someone who is not only teaching and initiating students in the First and Second Degree, but a teacher who is instructing others in the Third Degree so that they may in turn pass on the Reiki system in due course.

191 What is a Reiki Grand Master?

The term *'Reiki Grand Master'* is a term which is bestowed to the lineage bearer of the Usui System of Natural Healing and is a term held by the *Reiki Alliance.* The title Grand Master was bestowed upon *Phyllis Lei Furumoto* as the lineage holder of the system that was passed down by her Grandmother, Mrs. Takata. Although Mrs. Takata was not formally granted the title, the title of teacher (Japanese: *Shinpiden*) was conferred to her by Hayashi in 1938. In Japan, a teacher having served an apprenticeship with their teacher is granted the position *'Shihan'*, so it is likely that Mrs. Takata was granted this title. In her later years when Mrs. Takata began teaching students in America between 1970 and 1979, the titles *'Reiki Master'* and particularly, *'Grand Master'* began to be used.

In some Reiki circles, some Reiki Masters who begin to teach their students to be teachers choose to call themselves' *'Grand Masters'* of Reiki however this does not seem to be the norm. Another place where the title 'Grand Master' has gained wide-spread popularity is in India. I have heard of many teachers in India, using the term 'Grand Master' to describe themselves and their own Reiki teachers. After all, India is the home of the Guru and with a greater cultural emphasis on how qualified a teacher is in the grander sense is always an advantage for those teachers who are keen to secure many students. In other cases, it is a genuine understanding and matter of respect given by the teacher's students.

192 What is the Master symbol?

The Reiki Master symbol or the Third Degree symbol is one of the keys to awakening ones connection with Universal energy. This symbol is used during the Reiki attunements to transfer the Reiki ability in the student. For the Reiki Master symbol to be effective one needs to be initiated to the Third Degree by a qualified Reiki teacher. The most common Reiki Master symbol is the *Dai Koumyo*. It is depicted in traditional Japanese kanji and is successfully utilized in a variety of forms by teachers all around the world.

Other channelled or modern interpretations of this symbol can have positive effects, and in some cases little or no effect, so it is important that one has the correct depiction and transmission into this symbol for best results.

193 How is the Third degree symbol used in Reiki?

The *Dai Koumyo* is primarily used in the Reiki Attunement procedures but its use is not exclusive to this. The *Dai Koumyo* can also be used in distant healing or in hands-on treatments in order to bestow a greater and more concentrated amount of life force energy. Whenever the symbol is drawn by a qualified initiate, the energy field which is created is considerable when compared with the basic flow of Reiki energy. Of course the one who is signing or facilitating the treatment also has a large bearing on the amount of healing energy bestowed. In general, one can say that this symbol in particular, has the potential to awaken healing in profound ways. When used for the Reiki attunements, the *Dai Koumyo* is the connection to the Reiki energy. Its use in the attunement procedures creates a lasting alignment with the Universal Life Force energy. In effect it switches on a person's Reiki ability.

194 Can Reiki Masters give attunements without symbols?

In the original Japanese style of Reiki, one method of attunement utilises no symbols. This form of attunement is called '*Reiju*'. The Reiju process of attunement does not include the use of Reiki symbols nor does it employ visualization. It is a process where the teacher becomes one with the Reiki energy and then projects the life force energy to certain points of energy flow in the recipient, thereby bestowing an opening to the Reiki energy. In the Reiki Gakkai *(Japans Reiki Learning Society)* students attend monthly meetings or training sessions called: '*Shuyoka*'. At each meeting, whilst the students are practicing their energy practices called '*Hatsurei-ho*', they receive the Reiju attunements from the Sensei. Over time a student's Reiki ability will increase. Each time they attend they receive another attunement and over many months or even years, the students level of proficiency increases.

195 How quickly can a Reiki Master teach a student to be a Reiki Master?

Opinion to this question will vary from teacher to teacher, however I recommend that a teacher in training should have been actively practicing Reiki for at least two years before being considered for the Third Degree. Other teachers recommend at least five years.

For a teacher to pass on their own knowledge and guidance as a teacher in their own right, should be a considerably longer time. One need only consult their common sense to know that unless you have a sound understanding and direct experience in instructing others, then one can hardly be ready to teach another student to be a teacher.

As a general guide, I recommend a teacher of Reiki should teach the First and Second Degree classes for a period of at least three years, preferably five, before considering the role of a Senior Instructor. How can one teach others the ways of being a teacher, it they themselves do not have the experience of being a teacher? Sadly, it is becoming more common these days to see advertisements for becoming a Reiki Master in a one day workshop with no prior experience necessary. To make matters worse, one can even become a Reiki Master with the click of a button over the internet! One would think that people had more commonsense than this, but you would be surprised just how many people call themselves *Reiki Masters* after a quick visit to a website online.

196 Is there such a thing as group Reiki attunements?

As far as my research goes there is no traditional use of a group Reiki attunement. Meaning a teacher cannot give a lasting empowerment to a group of students just by standing in front of them and signing a few Reiki symbols. If anything a blessing can be given in this way but no actual transmission will occur. To illustrate an example, a few years ago there was a so called Reiki Master who flew into town one day claiming that anyone could become a Reiki Master with no prior experience in just one day! Over 100 people attended the seminar and the Charlatan in question stood in front of the class, made some hand motions and a minutes later announced that everyone in the room were now Reiki Masters! He subsequently flew out that night with over $150,000 in

Australian Dollars for one days work. Unfortunately, many traditional teachers (including myself), were left to clean up his mess, including the disillusioned and disgruntled students he left behind. Although his claims seemed genuine, the 100 or so unsuspecting spiritual seekers were none the wiser. As a result of his fraudulent claims, no actual Reiki alignment occurred. This is one of many examples where, under the banner of Reiki, misguided people take advantage of others. On the positive side, new standards are today being implemented to prevent this sort of thing in the future. Through educating the public through books and advertising, a more discerning message is now being broadcast.

197 Is there a global Reiki community or international head to Reiki?

If one does a search on the internet for Reiki, one will encounter thousands of Reiki websites. In amongst these sites one will find several international organizations for Reiki and its practice in the global community. If one is to say who is the international head or living successor of Reiki, aside from the many teachers who are self-proclaimed, one usually narrows the field to two Reiki teachers.

The more commonly recognised head of the Reiki Alliance is *Phillys Lei Furumoto*. She is Mrs. Takata's grand daughter and was placed in the position of Grand Master by her peers in the early 1980s. Another recognised head of Reiki, most popularised in the United States, is *Barbara Ray*, who is the spiritual director of *The Radiance Technique*. Although these teachers have created their own position on Reiki, the greater global community are the practitioners of Reiki themselves. Much like an extended family tree, once one is attuned to Reiki, one becomes apart of a larger lineage which has now grown in the millions world-wide.

198 Is there a difference between a Reiki Master and a Reiki Instructor and what is a Reiki Sensei?

Essentially, there is no difference in any of these names. At *The International Institute for Reiki Training (IIRT)* we use the term 'Instructor, Sensei or Teacher' over the term 'Master'. This is simply a matter of preference. The term 'Reiki Master', is used very widely in the Western Reiki traditions, though was never used by Usui, nor was it ever used in Japan. At the *IIRT*, we do not refer to our teachers as 'Masters' for reasons of humility, as the term 'Master' tends to create all sorts of ideas in peoples minds. The term 'Sensei' is the traditional Japanese name for a teacher, so we tend to refer to our teachers using this term. This does not mean that the person has supernatural powers or are some kind of 'Guru', it simply means they have completed the necessary training and have reached a place where they have the experience to pass this system onto others effectively.

199   Do Reiki Masters get sick or does their Reiki ability prevent illness?

Although it would be nice if it were true, Reiki Masters do get sick, they get old, and like everyone else, they all die. Now although no one is immune to illness, a teacher or student of Reiki can certainly maintain their health at an optimum level by attending to regular self-treatment and spiritual development. A healthy state of mind is important in order to stay well, but one should not smoke two packets of cigarettes and eat fast food, three meals a day either. A balance must be reached in every walk of life.

200   Can Reiki Masters avert their own Karma?

Much like our previous question, Reiki Masters, just like everyone else have things to sort out and some 'karmas' which play out in our lives are harder than others. One of the best ways to heal karma or avert the future seeds from sprouting is by doing good actions. The more one participates in positive activity in the things one thinks, says and does, the more we subdue the ripening of past karma and in turn the seeds for future positive Karma develops.

Certainly sending distant Reiki to difficult situations can be of benefit, as is making offering to those we have harmed in former lives. One simple meditation one can do, regardless of whether you are a Reiki channel or not, is to regularly do the following practice.

Think of all the harm you have caused in the things that you have done, said and thought from this life and former lives. Next imagine these past deeds as beings residing in your body. These beings represent all those you have harmed and need to repay. Make the firm resolve that you really wish to repay the harmful actions and with this, all of the beings spring forth from your body and stand before you. See these beings before you and now make offerings to them. Imagine that you are giving them every kind of worldly possession. Next imagine that you are giving them all of your best aspirations and love. Next imagine that you are offering even your body. Give them your organs, your blood, your life-force and see them receiving these qualities over and over. You finally stand before them, stripped bare. Having given them everything you possess, see that they are truly appeased. They now smile warmly at you and all karmic debts are repaid. With this, they return into your body, returning your gifts of every kind. You are left empowered and whole, feeling the deep satisfaction that all of the things you have done in the past to harm others has now been cleansed. Making the sincere wish that the good that has just been generated from your practice, benefits all beings, resolve to sow good seeds for the future. This ends the meditation.

Appendix

About the IIRT

The International Institute for Reiki Training offers traditional Reiki Training in a variety of styles and is regarded as being one of the foremost training Institutes for Reiki in the world today. The IIRT offers international training seminars for existing Reiki Practitioners and Masters, offering classes in Europe, the United Kingdom, The United States, Australia and New Zealand.

The IIRT also offers a Licensed Teacher Training Program for existing Reiki Masters who wish to establish a division of the IIRT in their country or capital city. For more information about the Institute visit: www.reikitraining.com.au

About the Author

Lawrence Ellyard has authored 4 books on Reiki and has been a teacher of several Reiki traditions for over twelve years. He established the International Institute for Reiki Training in 1996 and has trained over 30 Reiki Masters. He currently teaches and lectures on Reiki throughout the world.

Recommended Reiki Websites

The Internet is a wealth of information however it is good to know where to go in that vast ocean. The following are a list of recommended websites that cover an array of information about Reiki.

www.reikitraining.com.au *The International Institute for Reiki Training*
www.reiki.org *The International Centre for Reiki Training*

www.usui-do.org *Usui – Do*
www.reikialliance.com *The Reiki Alliance*
www.trtia.org *The Radiance Technique*
www.reiki.net.au *The International House of Reiki*
www.angelfire.com/az/SpiritMatters/contents.html *Reiki Ryoho Pages*
www.reikidharma.com *Reiki Site of Frank Arjava Petter*
www.angelreiki.nu *Reiki Plain and Simple*
www.threshold.ca *Reiki Threshold*
www.reiki-evolution.co.uk *Reiki Evolution*
www.healing-touch.co.uk *Healing Touch – Reiki Jin Kei Do*
www.australianreikiconnection.com.au *The Australian Reiki Connection*
http://reiki.7gen.com *The Reiki Page*
www.reiki-magazin.de *German Reiki Magazine*

Recommended Reiki Books

These titles presented here are but a few of the more useful books that I have read on the subject.

Reiki Healer, A complete guide to path and practice of Reiki – Lawrence Ellyard – Lotus Press
Reiki – Penelope Quest – Piatkus
Reiki – The healing touch – William Lee Rand – Vision Publications
Reiki – Way of the Heart – Walter Lubeck – Lotus Light
Reiki for First Aid – Walter Lubeck – Lotus Light
The Complete Reiki Handbook – Walter Lubeck – Lotus Light
Reiki Fire – Frank Arjava Petter – Lotus Light
Reiki – the Legacy of Dr. Usui Frank Arjava Petter – Lotus Light
The Original Reiki Handbook of Dr. Mikao Usui – Frank Arjaya Petter – Lotus Light
Reiki and the Seven Chakras – Richard Ellis – Vermillion
Modern Reiki Method for Healing – Hiroshi Doi – Fraser Journal Publishing
The Spirit of Reiki – A complete handbook of the Reiki System – Lotus Press.
Reiki for Beginners – David F. Vennells – Llewellyn

The Reiki Source Book – Frans and Bronwen Stiene – O-Books
   Publishing
Reiki – The essential guide to the ancient healing art – Chris & Penny
   Parkes
- Vermillion
Empowerment through Reiki – Paula Horan – Lotus Light
Traditional Reiki – For Our Times – Amy Z. Rowland – Healing Arts
   Press

Contact Details

To find more information about the International Institute for Reiki
Training, including Reiki training and our Licensed Teacher Training
program, visit: www.reikitraining.com.au
   On our site you will find over 100 pages on everything there is to
know about Reiki. Our site is globally one of the most comprehensive
and contains details on the Reiki styles and classes we offer, as well
as Reiki history; Reiki news; Membership opportunities; Online
Practitioner Directory, and details of where classes are held world-wide.
The Institute also runs seminar tours in your country, so if you would
like to learn with us, simply contact us from the website or write to us
at:

   The International Institute for Reiki Training
   PO Box 548 Fremantle 6959 Western Australia
   Phone: International +61 (8) 9335 1111

On a final note, if you find after reading this book, that you still have
more questions, please feel free to contact me and I will endeavour to
answer your questions.
   Who knows, they might even end up in a revised edition of this book
sometime in the future.

                                             Yours in Reiki
                                             Lawrence Ellyard

O

is a symbol of the world,
of oneness and unity. O Books
explores the many paths of wholeness
and spiritual understanding which
different traditions have developed down
the ages. It aims to bring this knowledge
in accessible form, to a general readership,
providing practical spirituality to today's seekers.

For the full list of over 200 titles covering:

- CHILDREN'S PRAYER, NOVELTY AND GIFT BOOKS
- CHILDREN'S CHRISTIAN AND SPIRITUALITY
- CHRISTMAS AND EASTER
- RELIGION/PHILOSOPHY
- SCHOOL TITLES
- ANGELS/CHANNELLING
- HEALING/MEDITATION
- SELF-HELP/RELATIONSHIPS
- ASTROLOGY/NUMEROLOGY
- SPIRITUAL ENQUIRY
- CHRISTIANITY, EVANGELICAL
  AND LIBERAL/RADICAL
- CURRENT AFFAIRS
- HISTORY/BIOGRAPHY
- INSPIRATIONAL/DEVOTIONAL
- WORLD RELIGIONS/INTERFAITH
- BIOGRAPHY AND FICTION
- BIBLE AND REFERENCE
- SCIENCE/PSYCHOLOGY

Please visit our website,
www.O-books.net